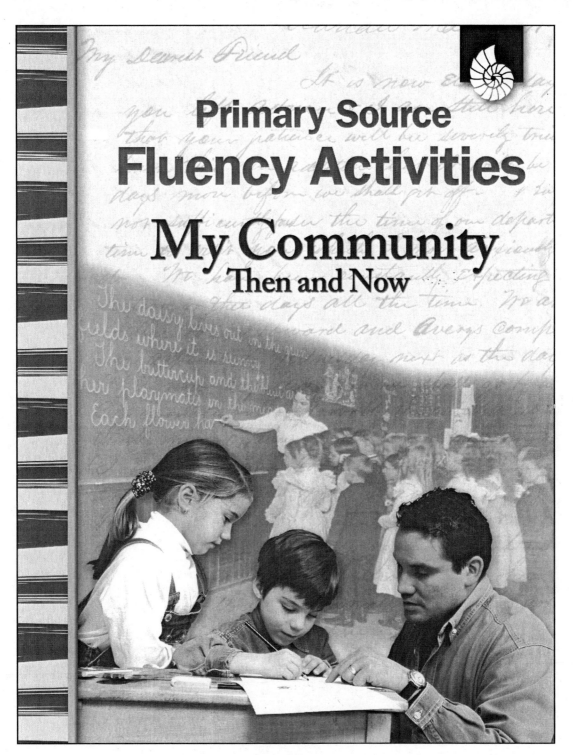

Primary Source
Fluency Activities
My Community
Then and Now

Author

Christi E. Parker, M.A.Ed.

Special Introduction by

Dr. Timothy Rasinski, Kent State University

SHELL EDUCATION

Contributing Poet
Dona Herweck Rice

Associate Editor
Christina Hill, M.A.

Assistant Editor
Torrey Maloof

Editorial Director
Emily R. Smith, M.A.Ed.

Editor-in-Chief
Sharon Coan, M.S.Ed.

Editorial Manager
Gisela Lee, M.A.

Creative Director
Lee Aucoin

Cover Designer
Lesley Palmer

Cover Art
The Library of Congress
The National Archives
Photodisc
Photos.com
Harold B. Lee Library

Imaging
Phil Garcia
Don Tran

Publisher
Corinne Burton, M.A.Ed.

Shell Education
5301 Oceanus Drive
Huntington Beach, CA 92649-1030
http://www.shelleducation.com
ISBN 978-1-4258-0368-7
© 2007 Shell Educational Publishing, Inc.

Table of Contents

Table of Contents *(cont.)*

Introduction to Teaching Fluency

By Dr. Timothy Rasinski
Kent State University

Why This Book?

This book was developed in response to the need we have heard from teachers for good texts for teaching reading fluency within the content areas. Within the past several years, reading fluency has become recognized as an essential element in elementary and middle grade reading programs (National Reading Panel, 2001). Readers who are fluent are better able to comprehend what they read—they decode words so effortlessly that they can devote their cognitive resources to the all-important task of comprehension instead of bogging themselves down in working to decode words they confront in their reading. They can also construct meaning (comprehension) by reading with appropriate expression and phrasing.

Readers develop fluency through guided practice and repeated readings—reading a text selection several times to the point where it can be expressed meaningfully—with appropriate expression and phrasing. Readers who engage in regular repeated readings, under the guidance and assistance of a teacher or other coach, improve their word recognition, reading rate, comprehension, and overall reading proficiency.

Students will find the texts in this book interesting and sometimes challenging. Students will especially want to practice the texts if you provide regular opportunities for them to perform the texts for their classmates, parents, and other audiences.

So, have fun with these passages. Read them with your students and read them again. Be assured that if you regularly have your students read and perform the texts in this book, you will go a long way to develop fluent readers who are able to decode words effortlessly and construct meaning through their interpretations of texts.

How to Use This Book

The texts in this book are meant to be read, reread, and performed. If students do this, they will develop as fluent readers—improve their ability to recognize words accurately and effortlessly and read with meaningful expression and phrasing. However, you, the teachers, are the most important part in developing instruction that uses these texts. In this section, we recommend ways in which you can use the texts with your students.

Introduction to Teaching Fluency *(cont.)*
By Dr. Timothy Rasinski

Scheduling and Practice

The texts should be read repeatedly over several days. We recommend that you introduce one text at a time and practice it over the next three, four, or five days, depending on how quickly your students develop mastery over them. Write the text you are going to read on chart paper and/or put it on an overhead transparency.

Have the students read the text several times each day. They should read it a couple times at the beginning of each day; read it several times during various breaks in the day; and read it multiple times at the end of each day.

Make two copies of the text for each student. Have students keep one copy at school in their "fluency folders." The other copy can be sent home for the students to continue practicing with their families. Communicate to families the importance of children continuing to practice the text at home with their parents and other family members.

Coaching Your Students

A key ingredient to repeated reading is the coaching that comes from a teacher. As your students practice reading the target text each week, alone, in small groups, or as an entire class, be sure to provide positive feedback about their reading. Help them develop a sense for reading the text in such a way that it conveys the meaning that the author attempts to convey or the meaning that the reader may wish to convey. Through oral interpretation of a text, readers can express joy, sadness, anger, surprise, or any of a variety of emotions. Help students learn to use their reading to convey this level of meaning.

Teachers do this by listening, from time to time, as students read and by coaching them in the various aspects of oral interpretation. You may wish to suggest that students emphasize certain words, insert dramatic pauses, read a bit faster in one place, or slow down in other parts of the text. And, of course, lavish praise on students' best efforts to convey a sense of meaning through their reading. Although it may take a while for the students to learn to develop this sense of "voice" in their reading, in the long run, it will lead to more engaged and fluent reading and higher levels of comprehension.

Introduction to Teaching Fluency (cont.)
By Dr. Timothy Rasinski

Word Study

Although the goal of the passages in this book is to develop fluent and meaningful oral reading, the practicing of passages should also provide opportunities to develop students' vocabulary and word decoding skills. Students may practice a passage repeatedly to the point where it is largely memorized. At this point, students may not look at the words in the text as closely as they ought. By continually drawing attention to interesting and important words in the text, you can help students maintain their focus and develop an ongoing fascination with words.

After reading a passage several times through, ask students to choose words from the passage that they think are interesting or important. Put these words on a word wall, or ask students to add them to their personal word banks. Talk about the words—their meanings and spellings. Help students develop a deepened appreciation for these words. Encourage students to use these words in their oral and written language. You might, for example, ask students to use some of the chosen words in their daily journal entries.

Once a list of words has been added to a classroom word wall or students' word banks, play various games with the words. One of our favorites is "word bingo." Here, students are given a card containing a 3 x 3, 4 x 4, or 5 x 5 grid. In each box, students randomly write words from the word wall or bank. Then, the teacher calls out words or sentences that contain the target words or definitions of the target words. Students find the words on their cards and cover them with markers. Once a horizontal, vertical, or diagonal line of words is covered, a student calls "Bingo" and wins the game.

Have students sort the chosen words along a variety of dimensions—by syllable, part of speech, presence of a certain phonics features such as long vowel sound or a consonant blend, or by meaning (e.g., words that express how a person can feel and words that don't). Through sorting-and-categorizing activities, students get repeated exposure to words, examining the words differently with each sort.

Choose words from a text that lend themselves to extended word family instruction. Choose a word like "hat" and brainstorm with students other words that belong to the same word family (e.g., cat, bat, and chat). Once a brainstormed list of word family words is chosen, have students create short poems using the rhyming words. These composed poems can be used for further practice and performance.

No matter how you do it, make the opportunity to examine selected words from the passages part of your regular instructional routine for these fluency texts. The time spent in word study will most definitely improve students' overall fluency.

Introduction to Teaching Fluency (cont.)
By Dr. Timothy Rasinski

Performance

After several days of practice, arrange a special time for the students to perform the text, as well as other ones practiced from previous days. This performance time can range from 5 minutes to 30 minutes. Find a special person (such as the principal) to listen to your children perform. You may also want to invite a neighboring class, parents, or another group to come to your room to listen to your children perform. Have the children perform the targeted text as a group. Later, you can have individuals or groups of children perform the text again, as well as other texts that have been practiced previously.

As an alternative to having your children perform for a group that comes to your room, you may also want to send your children to visit other adults and children in the building and perform for them. Principals, school secretaries, custodians, playground aides, and visitors to the building are usually great audiences for children's readings. Tape recording and video taping your students' readings is another way to create a performance opportunity.

Regardless of how you do it, it is important that you create the opportunity for your students to perform for some audience. The magic of the performance will give students the motivation to want to practice their assigned texts.

Performance Not Memorization

Remember that the key to developing fluency is guided oral and silent reading practice. Students become more fluent when they read the texts repeatedly. Reading requires students to actually see the words in the texts. Thus, it is important that you do not require students to memorize the texts they are practicing and performing. Memorization leads students away from visually examining the words. Although students may want to try to memorize some texts, the instructional emphasis needs to be on reading with expression so that any audience will enjoy the students' oral renderings of the texts. Keep students' eyes on the texts whenever possible.

One of the most important things we can do to promote proficient and fluent reading is to have students practice reading meaningful passages with a purpose: to perform them. This program provides students with just those opportunities to create meaning with their voices as well as the wonderful words in these primary sources.

How to Use This Product

General Information

This book contains reader's theater scripts, job advertisements, poems, letters, and songs. Activities for each lesson teach important fluency strategies as well as an understanding of different jobs within the community. Each lesson also contains primary source photographs. These photographs help students understand the changes and developments that have occurred within their communities over time. These photographs are available on the CD-ROM included in the book, if student copies are desired.

Depending on the reading levels of your students, you may find some of these pieces too difficult to use at the beginning of the year. Instead, focus on the pieces that have a lower reading level. This book is set up to help your students be successful and fluent readers. Instead of just reading the text once and moving on, the students practice and reread the pieces in preparation for authentic presentations. That way, not only does their fluency grow through careful repetition, but as the class discusses the pieces, the students' comprehension improves as well.

Presentations

One of the most important aspects of these lessons are the presentation pieces. The author and editors of this book have tried to provide you with plenty of ideas. If the idea suggested for a certain piece will not work for your classroom situation, flip through the book and look for other suggestions that might be suitable. The key is that you have the students practice reading the pieces for authentic reasons. If the end presentations are always just to their own classes, students will quickly lose interest. Once they have lost interest in the performance, they will not work as hard at perfecting their fluency. You will not see much growth in your students if they feel that all their practice is for nothing.

Instead, be creative and fun as you plan these presentations. Invite different guests, such as parents or administrators, to watch the presentations. Performing for other classes will give students the experiences that they need. Other classes make great audiences, especially if the content is something they are also studying. Keep in mind that many teachers cover the importance of being a member of a community, whether it is specifically in their standards or not.

How to Use This Product *(cont.)*

Presentations *(cont.)*

If you have a hard time finding people to whom your class can present, try to tie the presentations into celebrations or holidays. Some possible times to hold presentations might include Presidents' Day, the beginning of spring, Mother's Day, Memorial Day, Flag Day, the first day of summer, Father's Day, Labor Day, the beginning of autumn, Columbus Day, Election Day, Veteran's Day, Thanksgiving Day, and the first day of winter. Do not forget about celebrations that take place during entire months. Some of these include Black History Month, American Indian Heritage Month, and Women's History Month.

Finally, try to tie your presentations into school-wide events. For example, you could have your students add to the school's morning announcements. Or, you could ask for a special part in the Veteran's Day celebration. Rather than holding your own assembly, work with other teachers to hold a Poetry Celebration during which students read poetry. Remember, your students' fluency will only improve if you make the performances important and authentic.

Reader's Theater

Throughout the lessons in this book, you will find numerous reader's theater scripts. This is an exciting and easy method of providing students with the opportunity to practice fluency leading to a performance. Because reader's theater minimizes the use of props, sets, costumes, and memorization, it is an easy way to present a "play" in the classroom. Students read from a book or prepared script using their voices to bring text to life. Reader's theater has the following characteristics:

1. The script is always read and never memorized.
2. Readers may be characters, narrators, or switch back and forth.
3. The readers may sit, stand, or both, but they do not have to perform any other actions.
4. Readers use only eye contact, facial expressions, and vocal expression to express emotion.
5. Scripts may be from books, songs, poems, letters, etc. They can be performed directly from the original material or adapted specifically for the reader's theater performance.
6. Musical accompaniment or soundtracks may be used but are not necessary.
7. Very simple props may be used, especially with younger children, to help the audience identify the roles played by the readers.
8. Practice for the reader's theater should consist of coached repeated readings that lead to a smooth, fluent presentation.

How to Use This Product *(cont.)*

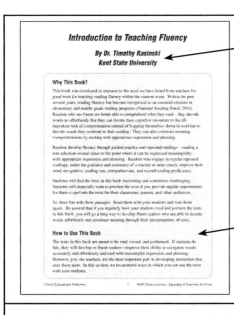

Introduction Written by Dr. Timothy Rasinski

- In a survey conducted by the National Reading Panel, fluency was determined to be one of the five research-based components of reading. Dr. Timothy Rasinski from Kent State University is an expert on teaching students to become fluent readers. His book, *The Fluent Reader*, is an excellent resource of oral reading strategies for building word recognition, fluency, and comprehension.

How to Use This Book

- Dr. Rasinski's introduction contains important information and ideas of how to use this book with your readers.

Objective

- A fluency objective is included for each lesson. This objective tells you which fluency strategy will be practiced within the lesson. See pages 13–14 for descriptions of the fluency strategies used within this book.

Fluency Suggestions and Activities

- These steps in the lesson plan describe how to introduce the piece to your students. Suggestions for ways to practice and perform the piece are also provided for your use. Remember that authentic performances are very important to ensure successful fluency for your readers.

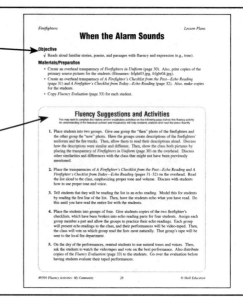

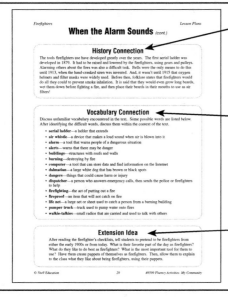

History Connection

- Each text in this book relates to a community worker. Information is provided with each lesson to give you the historical context of how the job has changed over time.

Vocabulary Connection

- Vocabulary words have been chosen and defined for your use. Introduce the words to your students and have them define the words or simply record the definitions on the board for student reference.

Extension Ideas

- One or two extension ideas are given for each lesson. These ideas are fun, challenging, and interesting.

How to Use This Product *(cont.)*

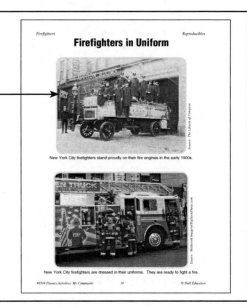

Primary Sources

- For each lesson, a copy of two primary sources is provided. These images are ideal for comparing and contrasting communities today with how they were in the past. The teacher can make copies of this page or use it to create an overhead transparency. These images are also available on the CD-ROM.

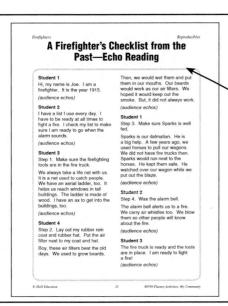

Fluency Texts

- The fluency texts provided are designed to be read and reread to promote fluency. The texts differ in strategy, but most are designed for students to work together in small groups or as a whole class. There are also reader's theater scripts for the students to perform.

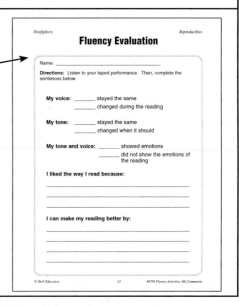

Fluency Evaluations

- At the end of some lessons, fluency evaluations are provided. Students can listen to a tape recording of their performances and complete the given forms. This is a great way for students to evaluate their own fluency.

Fluency Strategy Descriptions

These paragraphs describe the fluency strategies taught in the lessons in this book. These descriptions are meant to provide teachers with basic information about the strategies before beginning the lessons.

Call and Response

Call and response is a type of choral reading. When using call and response, one student reads a portion of the text and then the class (or a group of students within the class) responds by reading the refrain, reading the next lines in the text, or repeating the same lines as the reader.

Choral Reading

Choral reading is when groups of students read the same text aloud together. It allows for a lot of reading time by all students rather than single students reading while everyone else listens.

Cumulative Choral Reading

This is a special type of choral reading where one student begins reading. Then, at predetermined points, other students join in the reading. By the end of the passage, the entire group is reading in unison.

Divided Reading

Divided reading is used when dealing with a large piece of text such as a long speech, a short story, or chapters in a book. The text is divided into parts and read over several days by groups of students.

Echo Reading

In echo reading, one reader (or a small group) reads a part of the text. Then, the rest of the group (or class) echoes back the same text.

Oral Reading

Oral reading is when the students read the text aloud rather than silently. All of the strategies in this book fall under the strategy of oral reading.

Paired Reading

Paired reading is when two students or a student and an adult read text together. They can either read it chorally, or they can read alternating lines or stanzas.

Poem or Song for Two Voices

This type of poem or song has been written (or rewritten) so that it can be read by two readers. The readers alternate between lines while sometimes reading lines together.

Reader's Theater

Reader's theater is usually written for three to five students. It includes lines of a text that are read individually and lines that are read by all the students. It is like the script of a play, but there are few props and no costumes used in the production of the piece.

Repeated Reading

This type of reading is when the students read and reread a piece to improve upon their fluency. Every lesson within this book suggests that you have the students use repeated reading to improve their fluency before the performance of the piece.

Fluency Strategy Descriptions *(cont.)*

This chart indicates the fluency strategies practiced within the lessons in this book. Some lessons have more than one strategy marked because students will be working on multiple skills within the lesson.

	Call and Response	Choral Reading	Cumulative Choral Reading	Divided Reading	Echo Reading	Oral Reading	Paired Reading	Poem or Song for Two Voices	Reader's Theater	Repeated Reading
A Helping Hand	x					x				x
Directing Traffic		x				x				x
Fighting a Fire						x			x	x
When the Alarm Sounds					x	x				x
A Day at School						x	x			x
The Write Time						x			x	x
Dressed for Success						x		x		x
A Day on the Job		x				x				x
Get Well Soon				x		x				x
In the Operating Room			x			x				x
Library Time						x	x			x
Finding Books			x			x				x
Farm Work	x					x				x
Tools of the Trade				x		x				x
The Written Word					x	x				x
Extra, Extra—Read All About It!						x		x		x
Getting Money					x	x				x
Safe Keeping		x				x				x
Checking Out						x			x	x
Shopping Day						x	x			x
The Catch of the Day				x		x				x
A Day at the Fish Market	x					x				x
The Cleaning Crew			x			x				x
Swept Away					x	x				x
That's Entertainment						x			x	x
The World's a Stage						x		x		x
It's in the Mail				x		x				x
Trucking Around the Mail		x				x				x
The Votes Are In!						x		x		x
Running a Country			x			x				x
Scouting Out Ways to Serve						x	x			x
Guiding Others	x					x				x

A Helping Hand

Objective

√ Students will read a passage fluently and accurately using the call-and-response method.

Materials/Preparation

- Create an overhead transparency of *Pull Over, Please* (page 17). If preferred, print copies of the primary source pictures for the students (filenames: police01.jpg, police02.jpg).
- Create an overhead transparency of *What Is a Police Officer?—Call and Response* (page 18). Also, make copies for the students.

Fluency Suggestions and Activities

You may want to complete the history and/or vocabulary activities on the following page before this fluency activity. An understanding of the historical context and vocabulary will help students analyze and read the piece fluently.

1. Ask students what types of jobs they think a police officer has. Write the items they name on the board. Tell them that police officers do many things for the community. Display the transparency of *Pull Over, Please* (page 17) on the overhead. Ask the students what the police officers are doing in the pictures. Are they doing the same job? How have the jobs changed from one picture to another? What would happen if we did not have police officers in our community?

2. Place the transparency of *What Is a Police Officer?—Call and Response* (page 18) on the overhead. Read it aloud to the students. Model fluent reading, especially the use of tempo, as you read. Explain to the class that when reading, they should use the same pace. Their readings should be neither too fast nor too slow. Show students examples of reading too fast or too slow. Then, show them how to read using proper tempo.

3. Give each student a copy of the text. Reread the entire text together, as a class. Practice the reading several times. Tell students that you need volunteers to read the various parts of the reading individually (R1, R2, etc.) but the entire class will read the lines that are bolded. Have the class practice the call and response several times.

4. Place students into groups of six. Assign the members of the groups the various parts to read. Remind them to use correct tempo as they read. Allow the class to practice their call-and-response choral readings in their small groups until they become comfortable enough to perform the reading.

5. Tell the students that one of the groups will be performing the reading for the entire school on the intercom. Allow the groups to perform for the class. Then, let the class vote on which group should perform for the entire student body.

A Helping Hand *(cont.)*

History Connection

The job of a police officer has not changed a lot over time. Police officers protect us and fight crime. They make sure that laws are enforced. When the United States first became a country, there were not a lot of police officers. The citizens protected themselves. Sometimes, the military was used for protection. The first police department was started in 1618 in Virginia. The police officers protected the governor from American Indian attacks. Most police forces were not formed until the 1830s. They were started in large cities. Today, police officers are found all over the country. They use radios to talk to one another and to get information quickly. Most drive police cars, but some still ride horses or bicycles, just as they did long ago.

Vocabulary Connection

Discuss unfamiliar vocabulary encountered in the text. Some possible words are listed below. After identifying the difficult words, discuss them within the context of the text.

- **accident**—something not planned for that causes injury or death
- **citizens**—people who belong to a community
- **community**—a group of people who live in the same area
- **criminal**—someone who breaks the law
- **dangerous**—unsafe
- **enforces**—makes sure that laws are followed
- **evidence**—items found or collected which are used to create opinions or solve crimes
- **police officers**—members of the police force; people whose job is to protect the community and enforce laws
- **protect**—watch over; keep safe
- **testify**—tell what you know in court
- **traffic**—the number of cars or trucks on the road at the same time

Extension Idea

Allow students to find pictures in magazines or newspapers of ways that police officers help the community. (Or, have students draw their own pictures of police officers.) Then, have them create collages using the pictures they find, or create a large class mural using the students' pictures.

Pull Over, Please

It is the early 1900s. A police officer rides on his bike
next to a car. The car is not obeying traffic laws.

Source: The National Archives

The police officers today stop a driver who was speeding.

Source: Photos.com

What Is a Police Officer?— Call and Response

All: **What is a police officer? A police officer is someone who enforces laws.**

R1: They make sure citizens obey the laws. If citizens do not obey laws, they can be fined. They can go to jail, too. The laws are meant to keep us safe.

All: **A police officer is someone who catches criminals.**

R2: Police officers catch the people who break laws. Their job can be dangerous. They never know what to expect.

All: **A police officer is someone who collects evidence.**

R3: Police officers collect evidence at crime scenes. They collect evidence when there has been a car accident, too. They testify in court. They tell about the evidence they found.

All: **A police officer is someone who keeps us safe on the road.**

R4: They make sure we obey traffic laws. Sometimes, they give out tickets. They do this to keep other drivers safe.

All: **A police officer is someone who is seen in our community.**

R5: Some police officers are seen riding bikes. Some walk. Police officers can ride horses. They can ride motorcycles, too. But, most police officers drive cars.

All: **A police officer is someone who puts his life in danger to protect us.**

R6: They make our community a safe place to be. Police officers do a lot for the community.

Directing Traffic

Objective

√ Students will read a poem fluently and accurately within a choral-reading activity, focusing on voice and expressive language.

Materials/Preparation

- Create an overhead transparency of *Stop and Go* (page 21). If preferred, print copies of the primary source pictures for the students (filenames: police03.jpg, police04.jpg).
- Create an overhead transparency of *"Traffic Flow"—Choral Reading* (page 22). Also, make copies for the students.

Fluency Suggestions and Activities

You may want to complete the history and/or vocabulary activities on the following page before this fluency activity. An understanding of the historical context and vocabulary will help students analyze and read the piece fluently.

1. Tell the students that one job of a police officer is to direct traffic when it is necessary. Place the transparency of *Stop and Go* (page 21) on the overhead. Have students compare the two pictures. How are they alike? How have the police officers changed over time? You may choose to draw a Venn diagram on the board in order to compare and contrast the two pictures.

2. Read *"Traffic Flow"—Choral Reading* (page 22) aloud to the students. Model fluent reading, especially the use of expression, as you read. Then, place the transparency of the poem on the overhead. Read it aloud as the class follows along.

3. Ask the class what *expression* is. Tell them that the use of expression makes reading come alive. It shows the feelings of the reader. What emotions or feelings might be used in this poem? Is it a sad poem? A poem filled with excitement? Is it a serious poem? In what ways could they show the feelings of the poem as they read it? Discuss where certain expressions might be used in the poem.

4. Give each student a copy of the poem. Reread the poem together in a choral reading. Have the class use the expressions discussed as they read the poem.

5. Place students into small groups and have them practice the poem in choral readings within their groups. As a group, they should decide upon the expressions that they want to use as they read. Allow the class to practice their choral readings in small groups until they become comfortable enough to perform the poem.

6. Invite a police officer to your classroom to discuss traffic safety. Before the day that the police officer will be in your classroom, allow each group to chorally read the poem in front of the class. Have the class choose the group that did the best. That group can recite the poem for the visiting police officer.

Directing Traffic *(cont.)*

History Connection

One of the many jobs of a police officer is to direct traffic. Even long ago, police officers directed traffic. But, instead of directing cars, they directed horses with buggies. Today, if a traffic light is broken, police officers must tell the drivers when to stop and go in order to prevent accidents. They also direct traffic at the scene of an accident. Police officers must wear protective clothing when directing traffic, especially at night. Most officers wear reflective vests. They also use their cars' lights to let motorists know ahead of time to slow down. Often, traffic cones and flares are also used to aid in directing traffic.

Vocabulary Connection

Discuss unfamiliar vocabulary encountered in the text. Some possible words are listed below. After identifying the difficult words, discuss them within the context of the text.

- **beat**—the route or place a police officer patrols
- **police officers**—members of the police force; people whose job is to protect the community and enforce laws
- **traffic**—the number of cars or trucks on the road at the same time
- **whistle**—an object that makes a loud sound when blown into

Extension Idea

Before the police officer visits your class, have students prepare questions that they might ask the officer. Remind the students to think of questions that will help them understand all of the important things that police officers do for the community. They can also ask questions to help them understand the many job responsibilities that a police officer has.

Stop and Go

Source: The Library of Congress

This is a New York City police officer directing traffic in 1911.

Source: Andrew Barker/Dreamstime.com

A police officer today directs traffic on a busy street.

"Traffic Flow"—Choral Reading

People are moving here and there,

Walking and riding everywhere.

Traffic comes and traffic goes.

Where it's going, no one knows.

But, police officers help them go

By guiding traffic to and fro,

Blowing whistles and waving arms,

Keeping people safe from harm.

The whistle blows, "Tweet, tweet, tweet,"

From the old-time officers on the beat,

Who once wore dark and fancy clothes,

And helped horse buggies on the go.

Now, their clothes are in colors bright,

So drivers keep them in their sight.

Officers move the cars safely through,

And traffic lights help them, too.

"Time to go!" the officers cry.

"Beep, beep!" honk the cars, passing by.

"Stop!" officers call when the light turns red.

"Traffic's coming up ahead!"

Fighting a Fire

Objective

√ Students will improve expressive reading skills by engaging in reader's theater.

Materials/Preparation

- Create an overhead transparency of *Firefighters to the Rescue!* (page 25). Also, print copies of the primary source pictures for the students (filenames: frfght01.jpg, frfght02.jpg).
- Copy *Make Way for the Fire Trucks—Reader's Theater* (pages 26–27) for each student.

Fluency Suggestions and Activities

You may want to complete the history and/or vocabulary activities on the following page before this fluency activity. An understanding of the historical context and vocabulary will help students analyze and read the piece fluently.

1. Give students copies of the primary source pictures. Ask each student to choose one of the pictures. Have students write three sentences to describe the picture they chose. Then, allow them to find partners. Students should read their descriptions to their partners. Their partners should then guess which picture was being described. Display the transparency of *Firefighters to the Rescue!* (page 25) on the overhead. Have students share their sentences with the class.

2. Now, give each student a copy of *Make Way for the Fire Trucks—Reader's Theater* (pages 26–27). Before reading the script, point out the various punctuation marks throughout the script with the class. Ask them what an exclamation point tells them about how the sentence should be read. How do our voices change with question marks? Tell students to pay close attention to the punctuation as they read, to make sure that they use the correct expressions, in order to make their readings come alive. You may wish to review the use of expressions with the students at this time as well.

3. Tell students that they will be performing scripts about the firefighters in the pictures for another class. Since there are six parts, you may choose to assign different students the parts. Or, if time permits, you may choose to assign every student a part and then allow them to perform for more than one classroom, so that every student has the opportunity to perform.

4. Read the script together first as a class, choosing six students to read the parts. Then, allow students to choose the parts they wish to perform, or assign them their parts. Place them in small groups with the other classmates with whom they will be performing. Then, allow them to practice with their group members, paying special attention to punctuation, so they use the correct expressions.

5. Once students are comfortable with performing their scripts and using expression, allow them to perform for the class or, if possible, have them perform for other classes.

Fighting a Fire *(cont.)*

History Connection

The technology to fight fires has changed greatly over the years. In the seventeenth century, the first fire engines were created. They were simply tubs carried on wheels. The tubs were filled with water. "Bucket Brigades" were also used to put out fires. When a fire was first spotted, people would quickly make a line from a water source to the fire, with buckets of water being passed down the line. Then, women and children would race the empty buckets back to the water source to be refilled and taken down the line again. In 1725, Richard Newsham of London invented the first pumping fire engine. It was simply a manual pump used to force water through a pipe or nozzle. Today, there are several types of fire trucks and fire engines that are used to extinguish fires. The pumper truck is considered a fire engine because it carries water. It is the most common fire engine seen. The tanker truck is also considered a fire engine. It holds the most water, up to 1,000 gallons. At a fire, the water is unloaded into canvas "ponds." The pumper truck can then use the water in the pond to put out the fire. Ladder trucks are also used today. A 100-foot (30-meter) ladder with a bucket and nozzle at the end can be used to pump water onto roofs or high windows. If fire hydrants are not available, ponds or swimming pools are used to get water to the fire.

Vocabulary Connection

Discuss unfamiliar vocabulary encountered in the text. Some possible words are listed below. After identifying the difficult words, discuss them within the context of the text.

- **barrels**—large containers that store liquid
- **bucket brigade**—people lined up to pass buckets of water to put out a fire
- **buckets**—pails
- **buildings**—structures with roofs and walls
- **fire engine**—a fire truck that holds water
- **firefighters**—the men and women whose job is to fight fires
- **firefighting**—the act of putting out a fire
- **firehouse**—a place where the firefighters stay when they are not fighting fires
- **hydrant**—a pipe above the ground from which water can be pumped out
- **pumping**—moving a lever up and down to get water out
- **tanker truck**—a fire engine that holds a large tank of water

Extension Idea

Ask students to identify the different trucks shown in the primary source pictures. Then, have them create their own fire trucks, using at least one attribute from the "then" fire truck and one attribute from the "now" fire truck. The students should create pictures of their new fire trucks. Allow them to share their pictures with the class.

Firefighters to the Rescue!

Source: The Library of Congress

The firefighters are pumping water through a hose.
Other firefighters are bringing water in buckets. The year is 1733.

Source: Photos.com

Modern firefighters fight a blaze. They use their pumper trucks and ladder trucks.

Make Way for the Fire Trucks— Reader's Theater

> ### Characters
>
> Sparky, an old dog   Firefighter Ann
> Flame, a young dog   Firefighter George
> Firefighter Joe   Firefighter Sue
>
> **Sparky:** Flame! Don't you just love living in a firehouse? There is so much action!
>
> **Flame:** It is great riding in the tanker truck. When the alarm rings, I am ready to put out a fire!
>
> **Sparky:** You know, it was harder to put out fires when I was a young pup.
>
> **Flame:** Why? Didn't you get to ride in fire trucks?
>
> **Joe:** He sure didn't, Flame. Sparky's job was a lot harder. He had to ride on old wagons with barrels on top.
>
> **Sue:** The barrels were full of water. The water was used to put out the fires.
>
> **Sparky:** The ride was so bumpy! But, I liked watching the bucket brigade.
>
> **Flame:** The bucket brigade? What was that?
>
> **George:** Those were men who were lined up from the pond to the fire. They all had buckets in their hands.
>
> **Ann:** That's right! The buckets would go down the line. Then, the water from the buckets was thrown onto the fire.
>
> **Sparky:** And, I helped the women and children. I would carry the buckets back to the pond. They would be filled up again, and go down the same line. The firefighters did this until the fire was put out!
>
> **Flame:** Boy, that sounds like a lot of work! The firefighters did not have hoses to use?
>
> **Joe:** Not for a long time. The first hoses still had water pumped into them by hand.

Make Way for the Fire Trucks—Reader's Theater *(cont.)*

Ann: Now it is easier to get water to the fires. We get to use our pumper trucks, which carry water.

Sue: And, we have our ladder trucks. That way, we can reach the roofs of burning buildings.

Flame: Do not forget the truck that I like best! The tanker truck!

Sue: The tanker truck and pumper truck are called fire engines. That is because they hold water.

George: They hold a lot of water! Now we can get water to the burning buildings.

Ann: And, if we run out of water, we can use the fire hydrants to help us.

Sparky: One time, we had a fire in the country. Flame was just a baby then.

Sue: Are you talking about the time that we didn't have a fire hydrant?

Flame: No fire hydrant? What did you do?

Joe: We had to use the pumper truck. It pumped water from a nearby pond!

Sparky: That's right! We used the pond—just like in the old days!

Ann: We have had to use swimming pools, too!

Flame: Wow! I bet that was a sight! Pumping water from the pools to put out the fire! Good thing you had the trucks there to help you!

Joe: Firefighting has changed a lot over the years.

Flame: Boy, it sure has! I am glad that we now have tools to make putting out fires easier!

When the Alarm Sounds

Objective

√ Students will deliver a group oral presentation and read passages fluently with proper tone and volume using echo reading.

Materials/Preparation

- Create an overhead transparency of *Firefighters in Uniform* (page 30). Also, print copies of the primary source pictures for the students (filenames: frfght03.jpg, frfght04.jpg).
- Create an overhead transparency of *A Firefighter's Checklist from the Past—Echo Reading* (page 31) and *A Firefighter's Checklist from Today—Echo Reading* (page 32). Also, make copies for the students.
- Copy *Fluency Evaluation* (page 33) for each student.

Fluency Suggestions and Activities

You may want to complete the history and/or vocabulary activities on the following page before this fluency activity. An understanding of the historical context and vocabulary will help students analyze and read the piece fluently.

1. Place students into two groups. Give one group the "then" photo of the firefighters and the other group the "now" photo. Have the groups create descriptions of the firefighters' uniforms and the fire trucks. Then, allow them to read their descriptions aloud. Discuss how the descriptions were similar and different. Then, show the class both pictures by placing the transparency of *Firefighters in Uniform* (page 30) on the overhead. Discuss other similarities and differences with the class that might not have been previously mentioned.

2. Place the transparencies of *A Firefighter's Checklist from the Past—Echo Reading* and *A Firefighter's Checklist from Today—Echo Reading* (pages 31–32) on the overhead. Read the list aloud to the class, emphasizing proper tone and volume. Discuss with students how to use proper tone and voice.

3. Tell students that they will be reading the list in an echo reading. Model this for students by reading the first line of the list. Then, have the students echo what you have read. Do this until you have read the entire list with the students.

4. Place the students into groups of four. Give students copies of the two firefighter's checklists, which have been broken into echo reading parts for four students. Assign each group member a part and allow the groups to practice their echo readings. Each group will present echo readings to the class, and their performances will be video-taped. Then, the class will vote on which group read the lists most naturally. That group's tape will be sent to the local fire department.

5. On the day of the performances, remind students to use natural tones and voices. Then, ask the students to watch the videotapes and vote on the best performance. Also distribute copies of the *Fluency Evaluation* (page 33) to the students. Go over the evaluation before having students evaluate their taped performances.

When the Alarm Sounds *(cont.)*

History Connection

The tools firefighters use have developed greatly over the years. The first aerial ladder was developed in 1879. It had to be raised and lowered by the firefighters, using gears and pulleys. Alarming others about the fires was also a difficult task. Bells were the only means to do this until 1913, when the hand-cranked siren was invented. And, it wasn't until 1915 that oxygen helmets and filter masks were widely used. Before then, folklore states that firefighters would do all they could to prevent smoke inhalation. It is said that they would even grow long beards, wet them down before fighting a fire, and then place their beards in their mouths to use as air filters!

Vocabulary Connection

Discuss unfamiliar vocabulary encountered in the text. Some possible words are listed below. After identifying the difficult words, discuss them within the context of the text.

- **aerial ladder**—a ladder that extends
- **air whistle**—a device that makes a loud sound when air is blown into it
- **alarm**—a tool that warns people of a dangerous situation
- **alerts**—warns that there may be danger
- **buildings**—structures with roofs and walls
- **burning**—destroying by fire
- **computer**—a tool that can store data and find information on the Internet
- **dalmatian**—a large white dog that has brown or black spots
- **dangers**—things that could cause harm or injury
- **dispatcher**—a person who answers emergency calls, then sends the police or firefighters to help
- **firefighting**—the act of putting out a fire
- **fireproof**—an item that will not catch on fire
- **life net**—a large net or sheet used to catch a person from a burning building
- **pumper truck**—truck used to pump water onto fires
- **walkie-talkies**—small radios that are carried and used to talk with others

Extension Idea

After reading the firefighter's checklists, tell students to pretend to be firefighters from either the early 1900s or from today. What is their favorite part of the day as firefighters? What do they like to do best as firefighters? What is the most important tool for them to use? Have them create puppets of themselves as firefighters. Then, allow them to explain to the class what they like about being firefighters, using their puppets.

Firefighters in Uniform

Source: The Library of Congress   *Source: Credit*

New York City firefighters stand proudly on their fire engines in the early 1900s.

Source: Wollwerth Imagery/BigStockPhoto.com   *Source: Credit*

New York City firefighters today are dressed in their uniforms. They are ready to fight a fire.

A Firefighter's Checklist from the Past—Echo Reading

Student 1

Hi, my name is Joe. I am a firefighter. It is the year 1915.

(audience echoes)

Student 2

I have a list I use every day. I have to be ready at all times to fight a fire. I check my list to make sure I am ready to go when the alarm sounds.

(audience echoes)

Student 3

Step 1. Make sure the firefighting tools are in the fire truck.

We always take a life net with us. It is a net used to catch people. We have an aerial ladder, too. It helps us reach windows in tall buildings. The ladder is made of wood. I have an ax to get into the buildings, too.

(audience echoes)

Student 4

Step 2. Lay out my rubber rain coat and rubber hat. Put the air filter next to my coat and hat.

Boy, these air filters beat the old days. We used to grow beards.

Then, we would wet them and put them in our mouths. Our beards would work as our air filters. We hoped it would keep out the smoke. But, it did not always work.

(audience echoes)

Student 1

Step 3. Make sure Sparks is well fed.

Sparks is our dalmatian. He is a big help. A few years ago, we used horses to pull our wagons. We did not have fire trucks then. Sparks would run next to the horses. He kept them safe. He watched over our wagon while we put out the blaze.

(audience echoes)

Student 2

Step 4. Wax the alarm bell.

The alarm bell alerts us to a fire. We carry air whistles too. We blow them so other people will know about the fire.

(audience echoes)

Student 3

The fire truck is ready and the tools are in place. I am ready to fight a fire!

(audience echoes)

A Firefighter's Checklist from Today— Echo Reading

Student 1

Hi, my name is Jan. I am a firefighter.

(audience echoes)

Student 2

I have a list I use every day. I have to be ready at all times to fight a fire. I check my list to make sure I am ready to go when the alarm sounds.

(audience echoes)

Student 3

Step 1. Make sure the firefighting tools are in the fire truck.

I check the hoses on the pumper truck. I want to make sure they are tightly in place. We always have air tanks and face masks in our trucks too. They keep us from breathing in smoke. We take axes to help us get into the burning buildings.

(audience echoes)

Student 4

Step 2. Roll my fireproof pants down over my boots. Put my helmet and fireproof coat next to them.

I need to be fast when I get into my fireproof coat and pants. Every second counts when there is a fire.

(audience echoes)

Student 1

Step 3. Make sure the walkie-talkie works.

The walkie-talkie lets us talk to our fire chief. He warns us of any dangers. He gives us information about the fire, too.

(audience echoes)

Student 2

Step 4. Check the alarm. Check the computer, too.

When 911 is called, the dispatcher alerts us of the fire. Our alarm goes off. We check our computer. It will tell us the exact location of the fire.

(audience echoes)

Student 3

The fire truck is ready and the tools are in place. I am ready to fight a fire!

(audience echoes)

Fluency Evaluation

Name: _____

Directions: Listen to your taped performance. Then, complete the sentences below.

My voice: _____ stayed the same

_____ changed during the reading

My tone: _____ stayed the same

_____ changed when it should

My tone and voice: _____ showed emotions

_____ did not show the emotions of the reading

I liked the way I read because:

_____

_____

_____

I can make my reading better by:

_____

_____

_____

_____

A Day at School

Objective

√ Students will read passages fluently and accurately within a paired-reading activity.

Materials/Preparation

- Create an overhead transparency of *A Day of Learning* (page 36). If preferred, print copies of the primary source pictures for the students (filenames: tcher01.jpg, tcher02.jpg).
- Create an overhead transparency of *Learning Fun—First Person Narrative* (pages 37–38). Make copies for the students, as well.

Fluency Suggestions and Activities

You may want to complete the history and/or vocabulary activities on the following page before this fluency activity. An understanding of the historical context and vocabulary will help students analyze and read the piece fluently.

1. Display the transparency of *A Day of Learning* (page 36) on the overhead. Show students the "then" primary source picture. Ask them to list three things they see in the picture that are similar to their own classrooms today. Have them write their observations on pieces of paper. Then, show them the "now" picture. Have them write three things again from the "now" picture that are similar to their own classrooms. Place students in small groups. Ask them to share their observations with their group members.

2. Place the transparencies of *Learning Fun—First Person Narrative* (pages 37–38) on the overhead. Read the two narratives aloud to the students, modeling proper fluency. Then, read the narratives again, but with little attention to flow. Ask the students which reading they preferred. Tell them that it is very important to make reading flow. Explain to students that with practice, they can improve their reading flow and increase their fluency.

3. Next, give the students their own copies of the narratives. Tell them that they are now going to practice reading the narratives in paired readings. Allow students to find partners. Have them read their narratives with partners, with one partner reading the narrative first, then the other partner reading the same narrative again. Have them do this for both narratives.

4. Remind students to practice fluency as they do their paired readings with their partners, paying close attention to the flow of their readings. Now, ask them to read the narratives chorally with their partners.

5. Once students are comfortable with their readings, invite students' grandparents or older relatives into your classroom. Assign the grandparents to various partner groups. Allow the partners to do choral paired readings of both of the narratives for the grandparents to whom they have been assigned. Allow the grandparents to then share their thoughts about the schools they attended.

6. After students have performed the narratives, ask them how the narratives compare to the observations they made at the beginning of the lesson and to classrooms today. Would they describe the pictures the same way the students in the narratives did?

A Day at School *(cont.)*

History Connection

Schools in America have changed greatly since the first schools in the 1630s. The goal of the first schools was to have students learn to read and write, for the sole purpose of being able to read the Bible. In order to teach, one needed to be able to read, write, and attend church. Instead of pay, teachers received pigs, apples, or other foods. They also received firewood for the school's fireplace.

By the 1700s, few things had changed. Girls went to school to learn how to be homemakers. They learned to cook, sew, preserve food, and serve tea properly. Once boys were around 11-years-old, they became apprentices. They learned different trades.

In the 1800s, most schoolhouses were one-room schools. All students were taught together in the same room. In the frontier schools of the West, children did not attend school until November, so that they could help harvest their families' crops in late summer and early fall. At this time, teachers were being paid $4 to $10 a month. Schools taught subjects similar to those taught today, such as math, reading, and writing.

Most African American children were not allowed to attend school in the early 1800s. Some learned to read the Bible from white children. In the South, it was against the law to teach African American children to read or write. In the North, if schools did exist for African American children, they were always separate from the schools for white children.

In the early 1900s, children were spanked with paddles and rulers as a punishment. Not all children had the privilege of going to school. Some had to work in order to make money for their families. Most children who did go to school did not go past the eighth grade. They had to start working in factories or on farms. At that time, very few women went to college.

Vocabulary Connection

Discuss unfamiliar vocabulary encountered in the text. Some possible words are listed below. After identifying the difficult words, discuss them within the context of the text.

- **computer**—a tool that can store data and find information on the Internet
- **experiments**—ways to test ideas
- **history**—past events
- **knickers**—pants that end above the knee
- **manners**—a way of acting with respect toward others
- **memorizing**—a way of learning; keeping it in your memory
- **paddle**—a small, flat piece of wood
- **respect**—honor; admire; treat well

Extension Idea

Have students interview parents or grandparents about what schools were like when they attended them. How have schools changed? What types of rules did they have? What activities did they do? Then, ask the students to create collages of pictures (either drawn, from magazines, or real photos) showing what schools were like from the perspectives of those they interviewed. Allow them to share their collages with the class.

A Day of Learning

Source: The Library of Congress

Source: Credit

The teacher watches as a boy reads to the class.
Another boy does a problem on the board. The year is 1909.

Source: Photodisc

Source: Credit

Students in a classroom today raise their hands to answer their teacher's question.

Learning Fun—First Person Narrative

Then: Learning Fun in 1909

My name is John. I am in the second grade. The year is 1909. Miss Johnson is my teacher. I go to school every day. But, my older brother has to stay at home. He works on our farm. He helps make money for our family.

Miss Johnson teaches us reading, spelling, and math. She teaches us history and music, too. And, she tells us how to use manners. I have to be careful not to act out in class! I could get spanked with a paddle or a ruler. So, I always do what I am told! I make sure that I behave and follow the dress code. Boys can only wear pants or knickers. The girls have to wear dresses.

I like to read in front of the class. We do that a lot. We work math problems on the board. We do a lot of memorizing, too.

We have to buy our own schoolbooks. They cost a lot of money. So, I have to use some of my older brother's used books.

We do not have a lot of homework. There are too many chores to do at home!

My teacher takes care of our classroom. It is a rule that she has to scrub the floors and keep them clean. She has to put wood in the fireplace, too. Our classroom gets pretty cold in the winter.

I love school! The best part is recess! I hope that never changes.

Learning Fun—First Person Narrative (cont.)

Now: Learning Fun in 2007

My name is Ellie. I am in the second grade. It is the year 2007. My teacher's name is Mr. Jones. He is very nice. He lets us work in groups. He tells us to be creative. And, we go on field trips!

I love to paint in Mr. Jones's class. We paint pictures of the things we learn. We get to use the computer in our classroom, too. There are games on the computer to help us learn.

Mr. Jones helps us, too. He reads stories to us. And, he shows us how to do experiments.

We have rules in our classroom. We have to respect others. If we break rules, we do not get rewards.

I like going to art class and music class. Mrs. Smith is my music teacher. Mr. Wicks is my art teacher. They help me learn how to play instruments and draw faces.

I have homework. I use the books the school lends me. I take them home and bring them back every day.

I love school! Recess is my favorite part! I get to run and play with my friends.

The Write Time

Objective

√ Students will improve expressive reading skills by engaging in reader's theater.

Materials/Preparation

- Create an overhead transparency for *Writing Tools* (page 41). If preferred, print copies of the primary source pictures for the students (filenames: tcher03.jpg, tcher04.jpg).
- Copy *Changing Times—Reader's Theater* (pages 42–44) for each student.
- Make copies of *Expression Evaluation* (page 45) for each student.

Fluency Suggestions and Activities

You may want to complete the history and/or vocabulary activities on the following page before this fluency activity. An understanding of the historical context and vocabulary will help students analyze and read the piece fluently.

1. Have students walk around the classroom, looking for things they use to write and things they write on. Have them create lists of these things, including any type of art supplies. Discuss the students' lists as a class. Then, place the transparency of *Writing Tools* (page 41) on the overhead. Ask the students to examine the "then" picture. What is the student using to write? What other supplies are being used? Explain the picture. You may wish to refer to the History Connection (page 40) as you tell students about the picture. Show them the "now" picture. What is the student using as a writing tool? Which writing tools are easier to use? Why?

2. Ask the class what *expression* is. Tell them that the use of expression makes reading come alive. It shows the feelings of the reader. Write the following lines from the reader's theater on the board: "**Katie:** Humph! Write, write, write! Type, type, type! My hand is going to fall off by the time I get done with this assignment!" Read the sentences with excitement, then sadness, and then anger in your voice. Ask the students which expression would be the most appropriate to use. What other expressions might be used?

3. Give each student a copy of the *Changing Times—Reader's Theater* (pages 42–44). Tell students that they will be performing a reader's theater about a student who goes back in time. This reader's theater will be performed for other classrooms.

4. Read the script together first as a class, choosing six students to read the parts. Then, allow students to choose the parts they wish to perform, or assign them their parts. Since there are six parts, you may choose to assign only six students the parts, or you may choose to assign every student a part. If time permits, allow students to perform for more than one class.

5. After students have read the script, distribute the *Expression Evaluation* (page 45). Review the directions for the first section with the students, and have them complete it.

6. Place students in small groups with the other classmates with whom they will be performing. Then, allow them to practice with their group members, paying special attention to expression. Once students are comfortable with performing their scripts, allow them to perform for other classes. After their performances, have students complete the second section of *Expression Evaluation*.

The Write Time (cont.)

History Connection

Before computers, books, and markers were created, students used various tools to read and write. In the 1600s, there were no chalkboards. Teachers used sticks of charcoal to write. Pens cut from goose quills were also used, and it was the schoolmaster's job to make the ink. Lumps of lead were also used as writing tools. By the 1700s, hornbooks were being used. These wooden boards with handles had the alphabet, Bible verses, and the Lord's Prayer attached. They helped students as they learned to read. The top sheet of the hornbook, made of a bull's horn, was used to protect it. With books being quite costly in the 1800s, few classrooms could afford them. Students wrote on slates. Chalk was used on these hard boards so that they could be erased. Pens dipped in ink were still commonly used as well. Inkwells stored the ink.

Vocabulary Connection

Discuss unfamiliar vocabulary encountered in the text. Some possible words are listed below. After identifying the difficult words, discuss them within the context of the text.

- **alphabet**—the letters used to make words
- **arithmetic**—the study of calculating numbers; math
- **assignment**—a task one is asked to complete or perform
- **computer**—a tool that can store data and find information on the Internet
- **inkwell**—a small container that holds ink, used for dipping pens into
- **paragraphs**—the sections that a text is divided into; each section has a main idea
- **prayers**—words said to a deity
- **quill pen**—a pen made from a bird's feather
- **writing**—forming written words

Extension Idea

If possible, bring inkwells and quill pens to class for students to use. If inkwells and quill pens are not available, then bring feathers and tempera paint to class. Feathers can be purchased at most craft stores. Have the students write their names by dipping the feathers into the paint. Ask them if this method was easy. Did they enjoy writing this way? What problems did they encounter?

Writing Tools

Source: Eyewire

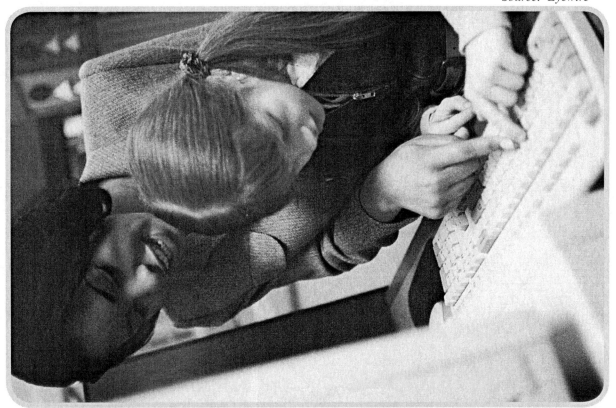

Computers can make writing easy today. A teacher shows her student how to use the computer.

Source: The Library of Congress

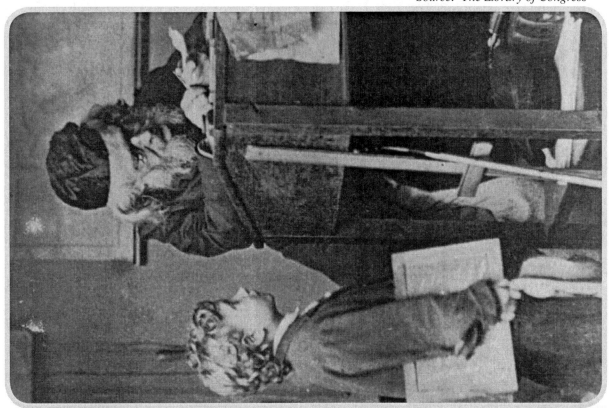

A teacher sharpens a feather pen as the student watches. The year is 1870.

Changing Times—Reader's Theater

Characters

Mr. Cash, a teacher from the 1870s   John, a boy from the 1870s

Katie, a girl from present day   Mrs. Lundy, a teacher from present day

Inky Inkwell, a magic inkwell   Narrator

Scene One

Katie: Mrs. Lundy, do we really have to write three whole paragraphs?

Mrs. Lundy: Yes, Katie. But, it won't take you long. You do have the computer to help you. Now, get started on your writing.

Katie: Humph! Write, write, write! Type, type, type! My hand is going to fall off by the time I get done with this assignment!

Mrs. Lundy: It is not so bad, Katie. Children in the past did not have computers to help them write.

Katie: I know. I am sorry, Mrs. Lundy. I will get started on my work.

Inky: Pssst! Hey, look down here!

Katie: What? Who said that?

Inky: Me, the inkwell inside your desk.

Katie: Inkwell? What is an inkwell? And, how are you talking?

Inky: I am an inkwell. I hold ink. Then, pens are dipped into me. And, I am not just any inkwell. I am a magic inkwell. I am from the year 1870. I heard that you were upset. So, you don't like to type on the computer, huh?

Katie: No, I do not! These writing assignments take me all day to do!

Inky: Well, your teacher was right. Students did have a harder time in the past.

Katie: They did? How do you know?

Changing Times—Reader's Theater *(cont.)*

Inky: They used me to write. And trust me, their hands got tired. Here, let me show you. Just close your eyes. Now, count to ten.

Narrator: Katie did what Inky said. In seconds, she was inside a classroom from the 1870s. No one in the classroom saw her. They were too busy writing.

Katie: Where am I? What is this place? What are those kids doing?

Inky: They are writing. Watch them for a while. Then, you will see what I mean.

Scene Two

John: Oh, my hand is getting so tired. I have copied the Lord's Prayer three times now. Dip and write, dip and write. I do not know if my hand can write much more.

Mr. Cash: John, be sure to practice the alphabet too. Then, you will need to get out your hornbook.

John: The alphabet too? Oh, my! I mean, yes sir.

Narrator: John completes his writing. He then takes out his hornbook. He reads the Bible verses found in it.

Katie: His hornbook? What is a hornbook?

Inky: These kids do not have books, like you do. They cost too much money. So, they used hard flat boards called hornbooks. The hornbooks have prayers and the alphabet written on them. That is how the students learn to read.

Katie: No books? Wow! That would be awful! And, did you see how long it took John to write his alphabet? Poor guy!

Mr. Cash: Students, it is time to get out your slates. We need to do our arithmetic. Be sure to have your chalk ready, too.

Changing Times—Reader's Theater *(cont.)*

Katie: Chalk? Slates? Did the kids get to write on the chalkboard? I love writing on the chalkboard!

Inky: Well, sort of. There is no chalkboard in the front of the room. But, each student gets a slate. The slates can be erased.

Katie: Well, that part would not be quite so bad. It would be fun to practice math that way! But, I have to say, I think I have it much easier back home.

Inky: You think so?

Katie: Oh, yes! I have markers, crayons, computers, and pencils. There are all sorts of tools I can use to write. And, my classroom has a lot of books. I am so lucky to have all of that!

Inky: Well, then! I think my job here is done! Now, close your eyes. Before you know it, you will be back in your classroom. No one will even know you were gone.

Narrator: Katie shuts her eyes. When she opens them, she is back in her own classroom. The first sentence she had typed is still on the computer.

Katie: Mrs. Lundy?

Mrs. Lundy: Yes, Katie?

Katie: I love writing! It is so easy!

Mrs. Lundy: You do? It is? But, you were just upset two minutes ago!

Katie: Well, I saw how lucky I really am! Now, I have some writing to do!

Expression Evaluation

Name: _____

Directions: Write two lines from the reader's theater on the lines below. Then, choose what expression you want to use for each line. Write down the expression. After you perform the script, check over your list of expressions. Did you use those expressions in your performance?

Section One

    1. Line One: _____

    _____

    Expression to Use: _____

    2. Line Two: _____

    _____

    Expression to Use: _____

Section Two

    1. Line One: Did I use the expression in my performance?   Yes   No

    2. Line Two: Did I use the expression in my performance?   Yes   No

    3. How can I make my performance better?

    _____

    _____

    _____

    4. What other expressions can I use?

    _____

    _____

    _____

Dressed for Success

Objective

√ Students will perform a song for two voices fluently with changes in tone, volume, timing, and expression.

Materials/Preparation

- Create an overhead transparency of *Nurses in Uniform* (page 48). If preferred, print copies of the primary source pictures for your students (filenames: nurse01.jpg, nurse02.jpg).
- Create an overhead transparency of *"Hooray for Nurses!"—A Song for Two Voices* (page 49). Also, make copies for the students.

Fluency Suggestions and Activities

You may want to complete the history and/or vocabulary activities on the following page before this fluency activity. An understanding of the historical context and vocabulary will help students analyze and read the piece fluently.

1. Give students blank sheets of paper. Have each student draw a picture of a nurse. Display the transparency of *Nurses in Uniform* (page 48) on the overhead. Show students just the "then" primary source picture. Ask them if their drawings had any similarities to the picture on the overhead. Have them state the similarities. You may ask them if their nurses were male or female. Then, show them the "now" primary source picture. Ask the students if their drawings had any similarities to the "now" picture. Have the class compare the two pictures. How have the nurses' appearances changed? How have they stayed the same?

2. Place the transparency of *"Hooray for Nurses!"—A Song for Two Voices* (page 49) on the overhead. Tell the class that they are going to read the song using "two voices" with partners. Read the song aloud to the class, so that they can hear it at least once. Then, point out the lines in bold. Tell them that those lines are meant to be read together with their partners. But, the partners should take turns reading the other lines. "Voice 1" should be read by the first partner and "Voice 2" by the second. Choose a volunteer to read the song with you. Read the song together, with you being "Voice 1" and the volunteer being "Voice 2." Be sure to read the bolded words together.

3. Next, give the students their own copies of the song. Tell them that they are now going to practice reading their songs together with partners, using proper tone. You may want to explain to them that the tone of their voices helps convey the meaning of the words in the song. For example, if the song is a sad song, their voices should be sad and lowered. If it is an upbeat song, then the tones they use should be exciting and upbeat as well. Have them use proper tones as they read.

4. Have students find partners. Have them read the song with their partners, with one partner being voice one, then the other partner being voice two. Remind them to read the bolded verses together. Tell them that they will be performing the song for nurses. When they perform, they can either read or sing the song. Give students time to practice their songs.

5. Then, invite members of the nursing staff at your school, or other nurses in the community, into your classroom. Assign the students different nurses for whom they will perform, or choose two to three partner pairs to perform for the nurses and the rest of the class.

Dressed for Success *(cont.)*

History Connection

There have been nurses for over 2,000 years. At first, most nurses were men. But, in the early 1900s, women took over the job of nursing. Nuns and the military were the two groups that mainly provided nursing services. Men were excluded from nursing in the military, therefore, women were the sole nurses during World War I and World War II.

The nursing uniforms have changed over the decades, too. In the early 1900s, most nursing uniforms consisted of full ankle-length skirts and tops. Aprons and hats were also worn. But, during World War II, the uniforms changed. With the need to conserve material, nursing outfits were reduced to one piece with short sleeves. Most uniforms were white. Uniforms of today are quite different. Nurses wear scrubs, lab coats, or even uniforms with pictures on them.

Vocabulary Connection

Discuss unfamiliar vocabulary encountered in the text. Some possible words are listed below. After identifying the difficult words, discuss them within the context of the text.

- **apron**—a cloth tied around the waist to protect clothing
- **comfortable**—feeling relief or at ease
- **heroes**—people who are admired for things they do or say
- **patients**—people under a doctor's care

Extension Idea

After sharing the historical background with students, ask them to design uniforms for nurses that would be comfortable enough for them to do their jobs, but also uniforms that will help put patients at ease. Allow them to draw and color the nurses' uniforms on blank sheets of paper. You may ask that they design uniforms for both male and female nurses, and combine the uniforms from "then" and "now" in their own designs.

Nurses in Uniform

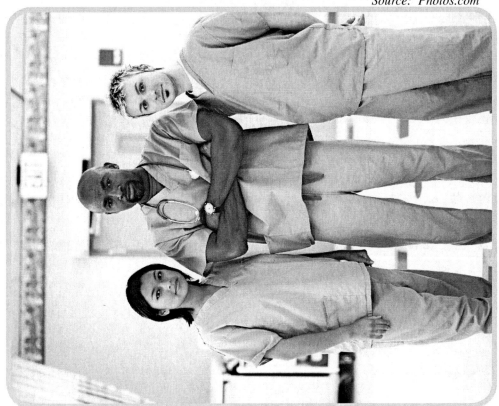

Today, both male and female nurses work at the hospital.

Hospital nurses get their picture taken in 1901. All of these nurses were women.

Hooray for Nurses!— A Song for Two Voices

Voice 1

Helping hands, helping hearts,

Nurses always do their part

To make their patients well and strong.

And so we join to sing this song:

Both Voices

Hooray for nurses!

They're heroes who care.

They work hard and long.

They work everywhere.

They work when they're tired,

They work when they're sad.

Nurses are heroes,

And we are so glad.

Voice 2

Helping women, helping men,

Helping others to be well again.

Whether long ago or today

Nurses come to save the day.

Both Voices

Hooray for nurses!

They're heroes who care.

They work hard and long.

They work everywhere.

They work when they're tired,

They work when they're sad.

Nurses are heroes,

And we are so glad.

Voice 1

Wearing the aprons of yesterday,

Or the comfortable clothes of today,

Nurses are heroes, tried and true,

And so, dear nurses, we thank you!

A Day on the Job

Objective

√ Students will read a poem fluently and accurately within a choral-reading activity, focusing on voice and expressive language.

Materials/Preparation

- Create an overhead transparency of *Helping the Sick* (page 52). If preferred, print copies of the primary source pictures for the students (filenames: nurse03.jpg, nurse04.jpg).
- Create an overhead transparency of *Putting Patients First—Choral Reading* (pages 53–54). Also, make copies for the students.

Fluency Suggestions and Activities

You may want to complete the history and/or vocabulary activities on the following page before this fluency activity. An understanding of the historical context and vocabulary will help students analyze and read the piece fluently.

1. Place the transparency of *Helping the Sick* (page 52) on the overhead. Ask the students to look at the "then" picture. Have them list three things that they find interesting about the picture. Discuss their lists. Do the same with the "now" picture. Ask the students if they had some of the same items on both lists. What things were the same about the pictures? What things were different?

2. Read *Putting Patients First—Choral Reading* (pages 53–54) aloud to the students. Model fluent reading, especially the use of voice, as you read. Then, place the transparency of the text on the overhead. Read it aloud as the class follows along.

3. Ask the class what *voice* is. Tell them that the use of voice makes reading come alive. The way a voice is used shows the feelings and emotions of the reader. Ask the class how they would say, "I am going to the nurse," in excited voices. Have them say it in sad voices. Then, ask them to say it using scared voices. Tell them that the way they use their voices can change the meaning of the sentence.

4. Give each student a copy of the choral reading. Explain to the class that they are going to read the text along with you. This is called choral reading. Reread the text together, in a choral reading. Have the class use proper voices.

5. Place students into small groups and have them practice the text in choral readings within their groups. As a group, they should decide upon the voices that they want to use as they read. Allow the class to practice their choral readings in small groups until they become comfortable enough to perform the reading. Tell them that they will be performing their choral readings for parents.

6. Invite parents to your classroom. Before the parents arrive, allow each group to chorally read the text in front of the class. Have the class choose the group that did the best. That group can recite the text for the visiting parents.

A Day on the Job *(cont.)*

History Connection

The first nursing schools in the United States were established in 1873. Before there were nursing schools, nurses were taught by doctors. At first, men were not allowed to go to nursing schools. The first school to admit men was West Penn Hospital. There are two main types of nurses: nurse practicioners and registered nurses. Both types of nurses have nursing degrees but nurse practitioners have more training.

Vocabulary Connection

Discuss unfamiliar vocabulary encountered in the text. Some possible words are listed below. After identifying the difficult words, discuss them within the context of the text.

- **comfortable**—feeling well and at ease
- **cuff**—a band wrapped around the wrist
- **degrees**—levels of schooling
- **hospital**—a place people go to get treatment when sick
- **illnesses**—sicknesses
- **licorice**—a plant with blue flowers and long, sweet roots
- **licensed**—qualified
- **medicine**—pills or syrup used to make you better when you are sick
- **midwife**—a woman who helps other women have babies
- **nursing school**—a place nurses go to learn about helping the sick
- **practical**—guided by practice
- **recipe**—directions for making something
- **registered**—recorded
- **syrup**—a thick, sticky liquid that is often sweet
- **temperature**—how hot or cold a body is
- **thermometer**—tool used to check body temperature
- **training**—system of learning skills
- **wound**—a deep cut

Extension Idea

After reviewing the primary source pictures and performing the choral readings, ask students to think of all of the things that nurses do. Then, have them create thank-you notes that could be sent to nurses, either in the school or at the local hospital. In the thank-you notes, have students tell why nurses are important.

Helping the Sick

One job of a nurse is to take your temperature. She uses a thermometer to do this.

A nurse visits a sick child in the 1940s. She takes the child's temperature.

Putting Patients First—Choral Reading

Time: 1865

A nurse came to my house today. We just moved to Oregon. There are not a lot of doctors here. The nurse is called a midwife. She helped my mother have a baby. She helps our family when we are sick. She has a recipe book that she uses. It has lists of plants that can make us better. She treats wounds, fevers, and illnesses with these plants. I do not like the cough syrup very much. It comes from a licorice root. It does not taste good. But, it makes me feel better.

Before we moved, we had a doctor. He had a nurse to help him. She made us feel comfortable. She gave us medicine, too. The doctor taught her how to be a nurse. But, some nurses go to nursing school. There are no male nurses, though. They are not allowed to go to nursing school. It is for women only!

Nurses help my family in a lot of ways. They make us feel better when we are sick. I am so glad to have nurses nearby!

Putting Patients First—Choral Reading *(cont.)*

Time: Present Day

I went to my doctor's office today. But, I didn't have to see my doctor. I was going there for a shot. The nurse gave it to me. He can help me a lot when I am sick. He gives me medicine. He takes my blood pressure, too. He uses a blood pressure cuff. He also takes my temperature. He uses a thermometer for that. The nurse always makes me comfortable. Even when I am getting a shot!

Nurses can be found in a lot of places. There are nurses in hospitals and doctors' offices. They can be found in nursing homes, too. That is where they care for older people who are sick. Nurses are even at schools!

The nurse at my doctor's office has a degree. That means he went to college for four years. So, he is called a registered nurse. Some nurses go through even more training. These nurses are called nurse practitioners.

Nurses help me in a lot of ways. They make me feel better when I am sick. I am so glad there are nurses!

Get Well Soon

Objective

√ Students will practice divided reading of a text in preparation for a performance.

Materials/Preparation

- Create an overhead transparency of *Hospital Rooms* (page 57). If preferred, print copies of the primary source pictures for the students (filenames: doctor01.jpg, doctor02.jpg).
- Create an overhead transparency for *A Home Away from Home—Divided Reading* (pages 58–59). Make copies for the students, as well.
- Copy *Flow Practice and Evaluation* (page 60) for each student.

Fluency Suggestions and Activities

You may want to complete the history and/or vocabulary activities on the following page before this fluency activity. An understanding of the historical context and vocabulary will help students analyze and read the piece fluently.

1. Display the transparency of *Hospital Rooms* (page 57) on the overhead. Show students only the picture of the "then" hospital room, but do not tell them what the picture is of. Ask the class what they think the picture is. Allow them to share their thoughts. Then, show them the "now" image. Ask students what the "now" picture is of. Tell them that both pictures are of hospital rooms. Create a T-chart on the board. Then, have the students list items found in the "then" hospital room. Do the same for the "now" room. Compare the items. How have the rooms changed over the years? How have they stayed the same?

2. Place the transparency of *A Home Away from Home—Divided Reading* (pages 58–59) on the overhead. Read the text aloud to the students. Model fluent reading, especially the use of flow, as you read. Tell students that when you practice the text, your flow improves, making the text easier to understand.

3. Distribute copies of the divided reading to the students. Also, give each student a *Flow Practice and Evaluation* sheet (page 60). Have students read the text silently, searching for unfamiliar words. Ask them to underline those words in the text. Then, review the directions to the *Flow Practice and Evaluation* sheet. Have students complete the first section.

4. Divide the class into four different groups. Assign each group a section from both the "then" and "now" texts. Tell the students they should read their assigned parts with their groups until they are comfortable reading their parts aloud to the class. Once they are comfortable reading their parts aloud, have the groups perform the divided reading as a class.

5. Invite a group of teachers, administrators, or aides into your classroom. Have the class perform the divided reading for the group. The students should then complete the second portion of the *Flow Practice and Evaluation* sheet.

Get Well Soon (cont.)

History Connection

Hospitals have changed greatly over the years. Long ago, people did not go to hospitals for care. Instead, the doctors traveled to the patients' homes. But, due to the often lengthy distance between the doctor and patient, many extremely ill patients died before the doctor could reach them. Today, people visit the hospital for both outpatient and inpatient care. The first nonprofit traditional hospital in the United States was established by William Penn in 1713. Now, the most common hospital is the general hospital, which deals with many diseases and injuries, and is equipped with an intensive care unit and emergency room. However, specialized hospitals also exist. These hospitals include trauma centers and children's hospitals.

Source: Credit

Vocabulary Connection

Discuss unfamiliar vocabulary encountered in the text. Some possible words are listed below. After identifying the difficult words, discuss them within the context of the text.

- **comfortable**—feeling relief or at ease
- **computers**—tools used to store data and find information on the Internet
- **hospital**—a place people go to receive treatment when they are sick
- **general**—not limited to one thing
- **measure**—determine how much there is of something
- **patient**—a person under a doctor's care
- **stethoscope**—a tool doctors use to listen to the heart

Extension Idea

After students have compared the two primary source images, ask them what they liked about each image. What made each hospital room unique or helpful to the patient? Allow students to share their ideas. Then, have the students create their own hospital rooms. What would they include in their rooms? How would they make the patient feel both comfortable and well cared for? Allow the students to design their hospital rooms on sheets of white paper. Then, have them share their hospital rooms with the class.

Source: Credit

Hospital Rooms

Source: The Library of Congress

A patient is cared for in his private hospital room. The year is 1895.

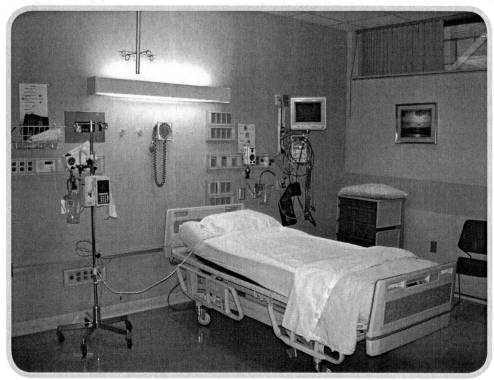

Source: Barbara/BigStockPhoto.com

Many tools can be found in a modern hospital room.

A Home Away from Home— Divided Reading

Then: 1895

Group 1

Welcome to Providence Hospital! You will be staying in a private room. So, you will not have to share it with other hospital guests. We will make you feel as comfortable as we can.

Group 2

You will find a large bed in your room. We have a sofa and chair, too. We want you to feel at home.

Group 3

Nurses will be here to help you with your needs. The doctor will check on you. He will want to see how your health is.

Group 4

But, you won't find many of the doctor's tools in the room. He keeps them with him in his doctor's bag. We have tried to make sure that your room is like your home away from home.

A Home Away from Home— Divided Reading *(cont.)*

Now: Present Day

Group 1

Welcome to Providence Hospital! We are a general hospital. We help people with all kinds of problems.

Group 2

Your room is not private. You may have to share your room with another patient.

Group 3

We have many tools in our rooms to measure your health. There are stethoscopes in every room. We can take your blood pressure, too. We even have tools run by computers! We want to be able to check your vital signs.

Group 4

We have nurses here to help you. All you have to do is push the call button. Let us know how we can help you. Our goal is to make you healthy!

Flow Practice and Evaluation

Name: _____

Directions: Write the words you need to practice reading fluently in section one. Practice the words. Then, perform the text. Did you have trouble reading any of the words this time? If so, write these words in section two. Keep practicing the words until you can read them fluently.

Section One

Words to Practice:

1. _____

2. _____

3. _____

4. _____

5. _____

Section Two

Words I Missed:

1. _____

2. _____

3. _____

4. _____

5. _____

In the Operating Room

Objective

√ Students will read a poem fluently and accurately within a cumulative choral-reading activity, focusing on voice and expressive language.

Materials/Preparation

- Create an overhead transparency of *Operations* (page 63). If preferred, print copies of the primary source pictures for students (filenames: doctor03.jpg, doctor04.jpg).
- Create an overhead transparency of *A Doctor's Note from the Past—Cumulative Choral Reading* (page 64). Also, make copies for the students.
- Create an overhead transparency of *A Doctor's Note Today—Cumulative Choral Reading* (page 65). Also, make copies for the students.

Fluency Suggestions and Activities

You may want to complete the history and/or vocabulary activities on the following page before this fluency activity. An understanding of the historical context and vocabulary will help students analyze and read the piece fluently.

1. Ask the students what items might belong in an operating room. Create a list on the board. Display the transparency of *Operations* (page 63) on the overhead. Show students the "then" operating room picture. Ask them if there are items in the picture that are not mentioned on the class list. Do the same with the "now" picture. Discuss the various items in the pictures and how they are used. Compare the two pictures with the class, discussing how the operating rooms are alike and different.

2. Place the transparencies of the two letters (pages 64–65) on the overhead. Read the first letter aloud. As you read, focus on the use of voice to show your emotions. Do this again with the second letter. Then, read the two letters in a monotone voice. Ask the class which reading sounded best. Explain the importance of using voice to show feelings and emotions when reading. Also, ask the class how the content of the letters are alike and different.

3. Next, explain to the students they are going to practice reading the letters in cumulative choral readings. They will be placed in groups of four, and each member will be assigned a number. Explain that R1, R2, R3, and R4 mean Readers One, Two, Three, and Four. The first reader will begin reading. The next reader will then read with him/her, and this will continue until the entire group is reading the text together. Then, one by one, readers will stop reading, until only the first reader is left reading the passage. Demonstrate this process with volunteers, using a stanza from one of the letters.

4. Give each student a copy of the letters. Divide them into groups and assign them numbers. Have them practice their cumulative choral readings, focusing on the use of voice. Tell them that they will be performing their readings for doctors in the community.

5. Invite a group of doctors to your room to discuss their jobs with the class. Have the class ask the doctors questions about experiences they have had in operating rooms. Then, assign a doctor to each group. Allow the groups to read the text to the assigned doctors.

In the Operating Room *(cont.)*

History Connection

As with all medical care, operating rooms have also changed over the years. Once called operating theaters, these rooms were semicircle amphitheaters that allowed students to observe medical procedures. The oldest operating theater was built in 1822 in London. The first public demonstration of surgery in the United States was in 1846 at the Massachusetts General Hospital.

Vocabulary Connection

Discuss unfamiliar vocabulary encountered in the text. Some possible words are listed below. After identifying the difficult words, discuss them within the context of the text.

- **anesthesia**—a medicine that causes a person to no longer feel pain in parts of his/her body
- **apprentice**—a person being trained to do a job
- **diseases**—illnesses or sicknesses
- **Hippocratic Oath**—an oath that doctors take, promising to treat their patients with respect and to do what is best for them
- **human body**—the body of a person
- **medical school**—a school that teaches about medicine and how to become a doctor
- **medicine**—something used to treat a sickness
- **operate**—to fix something on or inside someone's body
- **patients**—people under a doctor's care
- **scalpel**—a thin knife used in surgery
- **surgeon**—a doctor who can perform surgery
- **surgery**—an operation

Extension Idea

After reviewing the primary source pictures, assign each student either the "then" or "now" picture. Ask each student to choose five items from one of the two pictures. Have them find pictures of those items in magazines. (Or, have students draw pictures of the items.) Ask the students to create collages using the pictures of the items found in the operating rooms. They should title their pictures either "An Operating Room Long Ago" or "An Operating Room Today."

Operations

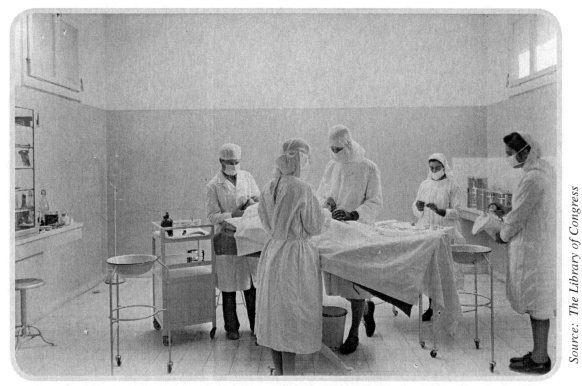

Doctors and nurses operate on a patient in 1940.

Source: The Library of Congress

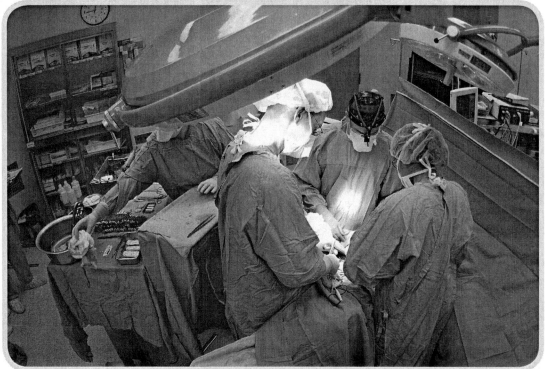

A light shines on the doctors as they operate today.

Source: Photos.com

A Doctor's Note from the Past— Cumulative Choral Reading

R1: Dear Friends,

R1, R2: I am preparing for my first surgery. I am a bit nervous.

R1, R2, R3: But, I spent a lot of years with Dr. Jacobs. He taught me everything he knew.

R1, R2, R3, R4: **I was his apprentice. I went with him as he cared for his patients. I know I am prepared to be a doctor.**

R1, R2, R3: Plus, I have all of the things I need in the operating room. All operating rooms have scalpels. They are sharp knives that surgeons use for cutting.

R1, R2: And, the patient will be given anesthesia. It is a medicine. It will prevent the patient from feeling pain during surgery.

R1: There are many other tools to use, too.

R1, R2: I can use the tweezers and forceps.

R1, R2, R3: These are called grasping tools.

R1, R2, R3, R4: **I must always wear a mask. I do not want to spread any germs.**

R1, R2, R3: No matter what, I will do what is best for the patient. I promised to do that when I took the Hippocratic Oath.

R1, R2: Yes, I know this surgery will be a success! I will write again soon.

R1: Your Friend and Surgeon, Dr. Scott

A Doctor's Note Today— Cumulative Choral Reading

R1: Dear Friends,

R1, R2: I am preparing for my first surgery. I am a bit nervous.

R1, R2, R3: But, I have had seven years of medical school.

R1, R2, R3, R4: **I took a lot of science classes. They taught me about the human body. I learned about diseases and medicines, too.**

R1, R2, R3: Plus, I have all of the things I need in the operating room. The X-ray machine will help me see where I need to operate. It has taken a picture of the patient's bones.

R1, R2: There is a large light in the operating room, too. It will help me see things better as I operate.

R1: I have many tools to use, too. The tools I use depend on the type of surgery needed.

R1, R2: I will have to use a scalpel when I operate. It is a cutting tool.

R1, R2, R3: But, the patient won't feel a thing. He will be given a medicine called anesthesia. It will put him right to sleep!

R1, R2, R3, R4: **I must always wear a mask and gloves. I do not want to spread any germs as I operate.**

R1, R2, R3: No matter what, I will do what is best for the patient. I promised to do that when I took the Hippocratic Oath. The oath has been said by doctors for over 2,000 years!

R1, R2: Yes, I know this surgery will be a success! I will write again soon.

R1: Your Friend and Surgeon, Dr. Goodwin

Library Time

Objective

√ Students will read passages fluently and accurately within a paired-reading activity.

Materials/Preparation

- Create an overhead transparency of *Using the Library* (page 68). If preferred, print copies of the primary source pictures for the students (filenames: lbrnns01.jpg, lbrnns02.jpg).
- Copy *Looking for Librarians Want Ad—Paired Reading* (pages 69–70) for each student.
- Copy *Expression Evaluation* (page 71) for each student.

Fluency Suggestions and Activities

You may want to complete the history and/or vocabulary activities on the following page before this fluency activity. An understanding of the historical context and vocabulary will help students analyze and read the piece fluently.

1. Place the transparency of *Using the Library* (page 68) on the overhead. Draw a large T-chart on the board. Write *Libraries from the Past* on the left side of the T-chart and *Libraries Today* on the right side. Ask the students to list things in the "then" picture that are seen in the library. Do the same with the "now" picture. Ask the class if there were any objects that were found in both pictures. How have the libraries changed? How might the jobs of the librarians changed, based on the two pictures and the type of technology seen in them? Have a class discussion concerning the questions.

2. Write an exclamation point, period, and question mark on the board. Ask the class how they would read sentences that end in exclamation points. Ask them the same about periods and question marks. Distribute copies of *Looking for Librarians Want Ad—Paired Reading* (pages 69–70). Tell students to pay close attention to the punctuation when they read the want ads, to make sure that correct expressions are used. You may wish to show students examples of how the sentences should be read differently when punctuation changes.

3. Tell students that they will be reading these want ads in paired readings. Each student will be placed with a partner. They should then read the want ads either chorally with their partners, or they should take turns reading the paragraphs or sentences of the want ads. Model this for students using a volunteer, paying close attention to punctuation and the use of expression and voice for each sentence.

4. Tell students that they will practice their paired readings with their partners. Once they are comfortable reading the want ads with their partners, they will perform the paired readings for the school librarian. If time permits, you may choose for all students to perform for the librarian. Or, you may ask just two or three partner pairs that showed the most expression and voice to perform for the librarian. You may also choose to evaluate students' reading using the *Expression Evaluation* (page 71) as they perform.

Library Time *(cont.)*

History Connection

The idea of a library has been around since the 1600s, with Boston, Massachusetts and Charleston, South Carolina having the first public lending libraries. However, the libraries were not free. Individuals owned libraries, and fees were issued in order to borrow the books. In the 1700s, Benjamin Franklin developed the idea of a subscription library, with people buying shares in the library. The money raised from the shares would be used to purchase more books. In other libraries, books could be rented by the day or hour. There were also "book boats" that traveled down the Erie Canal, allowing people to borrow the books at the rate of two cents per hour or ten cents per day. Later, libraries became free to all people, with taxes being used to pay for the expenses. This is how libraries operate today.

Vocabulary Connection

Discuss unfamiliar vocabulary encountered in the text. Some possible words are listed below. After identifying the difficult words, discuss them within the context of the text.

- **apply**—ask for
- **collecting**—getting; gathering together
- **college degree**—title people get when they finish college
- **computers**—tools used to store data and find information on the Internet
- **information**—a collection of facts
- **librarian**—a person who works at a library
- **libraries**—buildings used to keep books for people to borrow
- **magazine**—a paper book that has news and other articles
- **members**—people belonging to a group or club
- **newspaper**—a daily paper that reports news
- **organized**—orderly; prepared; structured
- **overdue**—past due; not returned on time
- **preferred**—liked better
- **schooling**—training

Extension Idea

After reading the two want ads and reviewing the historical connection with the class, have the students pretend as if they are owners of libraries 300 years ago. They want people to join their libraries in order to make more money. Have the students create advertisement posters, telling why people should become members of their libraries. Allow them to share their posters with the class.

Using the Library

Source: The Library of Congress

Students read quietly in the Library of Congress.
The librarian watches as they read. The year is 1899.

Source: Photodisc

Students work at computers in the school library today.

Looking for Librarians
Want Ad—Paired Reading

Date: 1800

Wanted—A Library Keeper

Job Description:

Do you like books? Do you want to be a part of the new libraries in town? Then, this is the perfect job for you. Your job will include putting books on shelves. You will need to keep the library clean, too. Books are free to members only. As the library keeper, you will be in charge of collecting dues. Dues are paid by library members once a month. Nonmembers may check out books, too. They will be charged two cents per hour or ten cents per day. You will also need to take the "book boat" up and down the Erie Canal. Here, people can rent books for an hour or for a day. Are you the person for the job? If so, apply today!

Schooling Needed:

No schooling is needed.

Skills Needed:

No special skills are needed. But, teachers are preferred.

Looking for Librarians
Want Ad—Paired Reading *(cont.)*

Date: 2006

Wanted—Librarian

Job Description:

Are you organized? Do you like to read? Then this may be the perfect job for you! The local library needs someone to be in charge. You will be in charge of story time. You will also teach classes. The classes will help those who cannot read. You will check out books to people. You will let people know if they have overdue books, too. You will need to help others find information by using the magazines, newspapers, movies, and music available in the library. You can also help them use the computers. Are you the person for the job? If so, apply today!

Schooling Needed:

You need to have a college degree.

Skills Needed:

You must be organized and willing to help others.

Expression Evaluation

Directions: Complete the fluency evaluation below concerning the use of expression. Place a checkmark next to each criterion that has been met.

Student Being Evaluated: _____

____ Uses punctuation as clues for type of expression to use.

____ Reads with expression throughout the passage.

____ Reads with enthusiasm when appropriate.

____ Varies expression to match his/her interpretation of the text.

Areas to improve:

_____

_____

_____

_____

Strong areas:

_____

_____

_____

_____

Finding Books

Objective

√ Students will read a poem fluently and accurately within a cumulative choral-reading activity, focusing on voice and expressive language.

Materials/Preparation

- Create an overhead transparency of *The Search Is On!* (page 74). If preferred, print copies of the primary source pictures for the students (filenames: lbrnns03.jpg, lbrnns04.jpg).

- Create an overhead transparency of *A Librarian's Letter from the Past—Cumulative Choral Reading* (page 75) and *A Letter from Librarians Today—Cumulative Choral Reading* (page 76). Also, make copies for the students.

Fluency Suggestions and Activities

You may want to complete the history and/or vocabulary activities on the following page before this fluency activity. An understanding of the historical context and vocabulary will help students analyze and read the piece fluently.

1. Ask students how they find books when they go to the library. What do they use? Who helps them? Display the transparency of *The Search Is On!* (page 74) on the overhead. Show them the "then" picture of the card catalog. Ask the students to identify the picture, if they can. Explain what the picture is, as well as how card catalogs were used. Then, show them the "now" picture. Ask them what the two students are doing. Write *Advantages* and *Disadvantages* on the board. Then, discuss both the disadvantages and advantages of using a card catalog to find books. Do the same with using a computer.

2. Place the transparency of the two letters (pages 75–76) on the overhead. Read the first letter aloud. As you read, focus on reading the letter smoothly. Do this again with the second letter. Explain the importance of reading smoothly. Tell students that through practice, they will be able to improve their fluency.

3. Next, explain to the students they are now going to read the letters in a cumulative choral reading. They will be placed in groups of four, and each member will be assigned a number. Explain that R1, R2, R3, and R4 mean Readers One, Two, Three, and Four. The first reader will begin reading. The next reader will then read with him/her, and this will continue until the entire group is reading the text together. Then, one by one, readers will stop reading, until only the first reader is left reading the passage. Demonstrate this process with volunteers using a stanza from one of the letters.

4. Give each student a copy of the two letters. Divide them into groups and assign them numbers. Have the students practice their cumulative choral readings, focusing on reading smoothly. Tell them that they will be performing their readings for other classrooms.

5. Invite another class to your room. Allow the groups to read the text to the class.

Finding Books *(cont.)*

History Connection

Searching for books in a library can be a tedious job. But, thanks to computers, finding books has become much easier. The first card catalogs were originated as lists often arranged by author. These lists appeared in published volumes in the nineteenth century. Then, in 1876, Charles Ammi Cutter, a librarian at Harvard College, developed the index catalog. Cards were used instead of volumes. One of his goals was to enable people to find books if the title, author or subject was known. He also wanted to show what books a particular library had, and then assist people in choosing the best book to use. He also developed the "Cutter Number System" to arrange books within a library. This system is still used in some libraries today. However, most card catalogs have been replaced with the online catalog. The Online Public Access Catalog (OPAC) is widely used by libraries today. This online catalog, developed in the late 1900s, aids people in finding available books at their local libraries. It can also be accessed from people's homes.

Vocabulary Connection

Discuss unfamiliar vocabulary encountered in the text. Some possible words are listed below. After identifying the difficult words, discuss them within the context of the text.

- **answers**—statements that respond to questions or problems
- **arranged**—put in order
- **articles**—pieces of news that are part of a magazine or other book
- **author**—someone who writes a book
- **computer**—a tool used to store data and find information on the Internet
- **index catalog**—a list of books and other resources written on small cards
- **Internet**—a system that connects computers around the world
- **librarian**—a person that works at a library
- **libraries**—buildings used to keep books for people to borrow
- **online catalog**—a list of books and other resources found on the Internet
- **resource**—material used to help find information, such as a book or website
- **subject**—topic
- **system**—a way in which things are arranged or placed

Extension Idea

Ask students to think about how librarians help them. How do they make finding books easier? What do they teach them about the library? Have each student finish the following sentence on a large sheet of blank paper: "A librarian helps me. . ." They should list at least three answers to the question on their papers. Then, have the students decorate their posters with things found in the library. Display the posters around the school to show the students' appreciation for the school librarian.

The Search Is On!

Source: The Library of Congress

A librarian searches for a book. She uses the card catalog to help her.

Source: Photos.com

Students search for books in the library. Today, they can use computers to help them.

A Librarian's Letter from the Past— Cumulative Choral Reading

R1:	Dear Friends,
R1, R2:	I have made it easy to find books. I have developed the index catalog!
R1, R2, R3:	Now, a list of books can be written on small cards. These cards will let us know what is in the library. We no longer have to look through large volumes.
R1, R2, R3, R4:	**The cards are arranged by subject and author. To find a book, you just look for the author's name. Or, you can look for the subject. Finding books will be so easy to do!**
R1, R2, R3:	I have three goals as a librarian.
R1, R2:	I want people to be able to find books.
R1:	I want to list the books our library has.
R1, R2:	And, I want to help people choose the right book.
R1, R2, R3:	My new index catalog will help them do just that!
R1, R2, R3, R4:	**Other items can be in the index catalog, too. We can list files and articles that the library has.**
R1, R2, R3:	My job will be to help them use my new card catalog! I have made a new number system, too. It will help people find the books on the shelf. I call it the Cutter Number System.
R1, R2:	Now, going to the library will be a breeze!
R1:	Your Friend and Librarian, Charles Ammi Cutter

A Letter from Librarians Today— Cumulative Choral Reading

R1:   Dear Friends,

R1, R2:   Have you heard the news? Finding books at the library is easier than ever!

R1, R2, R3:   Now, we can use the online catalog. This catalog is on the Internet.

R1, R2, R3, R4: **Just type the title, author or subject of a book. Then, the computer will tell you if our library has the book you need.**

R1, R2, R3:   We have more than just books! The online catalog can help you find articles, too.

R1, R2:   You can see if we have the resources you need just by using the online catalog.

R1:   Don't worry! We can help you use the computer.

R1, R2:   We will teach you how to search for books. That is a librarian's job!

R1, R2, R3:   Just think about all you can do in a library.

R1, R2, R3, R4: **You can find the books you need. And, you can find answers to any questions you have!**

R1, R2, R3:   Some libraries have robots. They help us get books from high shelves. Wow!

R1, R2:   New ideas grow and grow in our libraries.

R1:   Now, going to the library is a breeze!

R1, R2:   Your Librarians, Ann Smith and Dan Thomas

Farm Work

Objective

√ Students will read a passage fluently and accurately using the call-and-response method.

Materials/Preparation

- Create an overhead transparency of *Plowing Away* (page 79). If preferred, print copies of the primary source pictures for your students (filenames: farmer01.jpg, farmer02.jpg).

- Create an overhead transparency of *"My Trusty Plow"—Call and Response* (page 80). Also, make copies for the students.

Fluency Suggestions and Activities

You may want to complete the history and/or vocabulary activities on the following page before this fluency activity. An understanding of the historical context and vocabulary will help students analyze and read the piece fluently.

1. Create a large Venn diagram on the board. Then, show students the two pictures of the plows by placing the transparency of *Plowing Away* (page 79) on the overhead. Ask the class what they notice about the "then" plow. Write their observations in the correct portion of the Venn diagram. Do the same with the "now" plow. Have students then list things that the two plows have in common. Discuss the changes from the "then" plow to the "now" plow with the class.

2. Read *"My Trusty Plow"—Call and Response* (page 80) aloud to the students. Model fluent reading, especially the use of flow and proper phrasing, as you read. Then, read the poem once again, but this time, pause where it is not necessary. Ask the students what they noticed about the second reading. Explain to the class that it is important to have proper flow and phrasing when reading. Remind them that the best way to make sure that they have proper flow is to practice their readings.

3. Give each student a copy of the poem. Reread the poem as a class. Practice the reading several times. Then, tell students that you need volunteers to read the various parts of the reading. Assign the volunteers the different reading parts from the poem. Explain that the entire class will still read the lines that are bolded. Have the class practice the call and response several times.

4. Place students into groups of six. Assign the members of the groups the various parts to read. Remind them to pay attention to how their reading flows. Allow the class to practice their call-and-response readings in their small groups until they become comfortable enough to perform the poem. Tell the class that one group will be performing the poem for the principal and other school officials.

5. After practicing, allow the groups to perform for the class. Then, let the class vote on which group should perform for the principal and school officials. Invite the principal and school officials to your classroom for the performance.

Farm Work *(cont.)*

History Connection

Plows are essential tools for farming. Fields have been plowed for over 2,000 years. Plows break up soil and make the land ready for planting crops. Egyptians were the first to use plow-like tools that were pulled by oxen. These first plows were made of wood and stone. In 1819, Jethro Wood invented an iron plow with interchangeable parts. And, in 1837, John Deere created a steel plow, which was much stronger than the wooden plow. These plows were pulled by oxen or horses. Today, plows are pulled by tractors.

Vocabulary Connection

Discuss unfamiliar vocabulary encountered in the text. Some possible words are listed below. After identifying the difficult words, discuss them within the context of the text.

- **fertile**—able to produce a large number of plants
- **furrow**—a long trench in the ground; ditch
- **motorized**—having a motor
- **sow**—to put seeds in the ground
- **trample**—stomp on

Extension Idea

After sharing the historical information, pictures, and poem with the class, ask the students to think about how a plow works. Then, give the class art supplies and blank sheets of paper. What do plows do to make a farmer's job easier? Have students create illustrations, showing how plows help farmers.

Plowing Away

Source: The Library of Congress

It is time to plant crops! A farmer uses a plow to help him.
It is pulled by horses. The year is 1917.

Source: Art Explosion

A farmer and his workers plow the fields. The modern plow makes
it easy for them to pick crops. The plow is pulled by a tractor.

"My Trusty Plow"—Call and Response

R1: The land I work is fertile.

The soil's rich and deep.

I'll plant my crops with a hopeful heart

All: And faithful watch I'll keep.

R2: But, first I must make ready

The good brown earth to sow.

With some luck and loving care

All: A healthy crop will grow.

R3: So, across the earth I trample,

My trusty plow in hand.

I turn the rich brown soil

All: And dig furrows in the land.

R4: In times past, I'd trail my plow

Pulled by ox or mule or horse.

But now my plow is motorized

All: And on top I ride, of course.

R5: And once the ground is ready,

And my plow has done its deed,

The seeds I'll plant with care

All: And water all they need.

R6: Then time will do its magic

And my precious seeds will sprout,

Because I started carefully

All: With my plow to help me out.

Tools of the Trade

Objective

√ Students will practice divided reading of a text in preparation for a performance.

Materials/Preparation

- Create an overhead transparency of *Planting the Seeds* (page 83). If preferred, print copies of the primary source pictures for the students (filenames: farmer03.jpg, farmer04.jpg).
- Create an overhead transparency of *Time to Seed—Divided Reading* (pages 84–85). Also, make copies for the students.

Fluency Suggestions and Activities

You may want to complete the history and/or vocabulary activities on the following page before this fluency activity. An understanding of the historical context and vocabulary will help students analyze and read the piece fluently.

1. Ask students to close their eyes and pretend to be farmers. They have thousands of seeds to plant. How will they do this? What tools will they use? Will they have animals help them? Will they need animals to help them? Allow students to share some of their thoughts and images that came to mind. You may even ask them to draw pictures of how they would complete the job. Then, display *Planting the Seeds* (page 83) on the overhead. How did their images compare to the photographs? Which technique looks easier—the technique from the "then" picture or the "now" picture? How and why? How do the two techniques differ? How are they the same?

2. Distribute *Time to Seed—Divided Reading* (pages 84–85) to the class. Review the text with the students, using the overhead transparency. Point out any difficult words. Then, read the text aloud to the class. Tell the students that as they read the text, they are going to focus on volume. Read the text once again, but in a quiet voice. Then, do so in a loud voice. Ask the class if they liked the way the text was read. Explain to them that they should change their volume with the expressions in the text. If someone is excited, his or her voice may get loud. But, if someone is sad or calm, his/her voice would be soft and quiet. Go over other examples of when to use different volumes when reading a text.

3. Place the students into four groups. Have students reread the text in their groups. Then, assign each group a part of the text for both the "then" and "now" reading. Explain that the entire class will be performing a divided reading. Tell them that they will read the text together as a group when it is their group's turn. Allow them to practice reading their assigned parts with their groups.

4. Once students have read the text within their groups, practicing appropriate volume, have the class perform the text, with the groups reading their assigned parts. Then, tell them that they are going to read the text for grandparents. Invite students' grandparents or older relatives to your classroom. Allow the class to perform the divided reading aloud for the special guests.

Tools of the Trade *(cont.)*

History Connection

Farming tools have evolved over time. Before combines, tractors were mainly used to do the majority of work on farms. The tractors pulled machines that were used for tilling and planting. Tractors are still used on the majority of farms today. But, before tractors, farmers had to use animals and their own hands to plant crops. It wasn't until the early 1700s that Jethro Tull invented the seed drill. This drill allowed farmers to sow seeds in evenly placed rows. Before the seed drill, farmers randomly threw seeds, with less control over where the seeds would grow. The simple throwing of seeds was called *broadcasting*. The advancements in farm machinery have allowed for more crops to be planted in a lesser amount of time and at greater depths.

Vocabulary Connection

Discuss unfamiliar vocabulary encountered in the text. Some possible words are listed below. After identifying the difficult words, discuss them within the context of the text.

- **broadcasting**—planting seeds by randomly placing them in the ground
- **combine**—a machine that picks and threshes grain over a large field
- **fertilize**—to add nutrients to the soil to help a plant grow
- **machine**—a device used to help people complete a task
- **tractor**—a vehicle with large wheels, used on farms to pull other machines

Extension Idea

Tell students that there are many tools found on farms. Give the class magazines and newspapers and ask the students to find pictures of tools that might be found on a farm. (Or, have students draw pictures of different tools.) Have the students create collages of these farm pictures. As a class, discuss the various tools the students found.

Planting the Seeds

Source: Photos.com

An ox helps a farmer in Asia. The ox pulls
the seeding tool. One row is planted at a time.

Source: Photos.com

A tractor pulls a seeding machine.
Many rows of seeds are planted at the same time.

Time to Seed—Divided Reading

Then

Group 1

I am a farmer. Today, I am going to plant seeds. My ox, Old Brown, is going to help me. The land has been plowed. Now, seeds can be planted. Old Brown helps me plant the seeds by pulling the seeding tool.

Group 2

There are a lot of tools we can use to plant seeds. I use the seed drill. It is easy for Old Brown to pull! The seed drill lets me plant seeds in even rows. But, I can only do one row at a time.

Group 3

Before the seed drill, farmers planted seeds by hand. They just threw the seeds on the soil. This was called broadcasting. It did not work as well as the seed drill. The drill lets us plant seeds deeper into the ground.

Group 4

The seed drill helps me plant my seeds. It helps my plants have a better chance to grow because the seeds are planted deep in the soil. I am thankful for the farming tools I have.

Time to Seed—Divided Reading *(cont.)*

Now

Group 1

I am a farmer. Today, I am going to plant seeds. I use my tractor to pull the seeding machine. I do not have to plow my field first. The seeding machine does that for me as it plants the seeds.

Group 2

A lot of seeds can be planted this way. The seeding machine plants two or three rows of seeds at the same time. Thanks to my machine, a lot of plants are grown. And, it does not take a lot of time!

Group 3

After the seeds are planted, I fertilize them. The fertilizer will help them grow. The plants are watered, too. Then, once they grow, I use a combine to gather the crops.

Group 4

Thanks to my tractor and these seeding machines, I can plant a lot of seeds. And, it does not take me as long as it would have without these machines. I am thankful for the farming tools I have.

The Written Word

Objective

√ Students will deliver a group oral presentation and read passages fluently with proper tone and volume using echo reading.

Materials/Preparation

- Create an overhead transparency of *Write Away* (page 88). If preferred, print copies of the primary source pictures for the students (filenames: writer01.jpg, writer02.jpg).

- Create an overhead transparency of *Typing Away—An Echo Reading from the Past* (page 89) and *Typing Away—An Echo Reading from Today* (pages 90–91). Also, make copies for the students.

Fluency Suggestions and Activities

You may want to complete the history and/or vocabulary activities on the following page before this fluency activity. An understanding of the historical context and vocabulary will help students analyze and read the piece fluently.

1. Display the transparency of *Write Away* (page 88) on the overhead. Create a T-chart on the board. Write *typewriter* above the first section and *laptop* above the second. Have the class list observations from the photos about both writing tools. Write their observations under the appropriate categories on the T-chart. Then, discuss with the class how the writing tools differ and how they are the same.

2. Place the transparencies of *Typing Away—An Echo Reading from the Past* and *Typing Away—An Echo Reading from Today* (pages 89–91) on the overhead. Read the echo reading aloud to students. Model the use of tone as you read.

3. Next, give the students their own copies of the reading. Tell them that they are now going to practice reading in small groups. They will be performing echo readings with their groups. Explain how to perform an echo reading by asking volunteers to echo what you read. Assign the volunteers the student parts, and model the echo reading for the rest of the class. Then, place the students into their small groups.

4. Have students practice their readings in their small groups. Stress the use of tone as they read. You may want to explain to them that the tone of their voices conveys the meaning of the words in the reading. How do the speakers feel in the readings? Have them use the correct tones to show the feelings from the echo reading. You may wish to practice various tones before the students practice their echo readings.

5. Tell them that they will be performing the echo reading for other teachers or administrators. Allow students time to practice their echo readings.

6. Then, invite the special guests to the classroom. Allow the groups to perform for the teachers and administrators, or allow the entire class to perform in one large echo reading.

The Written Word *(cont.)*

History Connection

The first modern typewriter was created in 1866 by Christopher Latham Sholes. He and his partners created the first practical typewriter, which was manufactured by the Remington Arms Company in 1873. The biggest problem with the typewriter was that the keys often jammed. Today, our computers still use the universal keyboard from that typewriter. It is difficult to pinpoint the first laptop computer. Many say that Manny Fernandez created the laptop for executives to use in May 1983. But, other historians claim that the first true laptop was the Osborne 1, a portable computer weighing 24 pounds (11 kg), that was created by Adam Osborne in 1981.

Vocabulary Connection

Discuss unfamiliar vocabulary encountered in the text. Some possible words are listed below. After identifying the difficult words, discuss them within the context of the text.

- **blog**—a shorter name for a weblog
- **carved**—engraved or cut by chipping away
- **computer**—a tool used to store data and find information on the Internet
- **email**—a shorter name for electronic mail
- **electronic mail**—a system where computer users can create mail on their computers and send it to other computers in a matter of seconds
- **Internet**—a system that connects computers around the world
- **keyboard**—a typing tool that has rows of keys with letters on them; used to form words on both typewriters and computers
- **papyrus**—a plant used to make paper in ancient Egypt
- **styluses**—pointed tools used to write
- **typewriter**—a writing tool that forms words by striking one letter at a time
- **weblogs**—journals found on the Internet
- **websites**—addresses found on the Internet that show a series of pages
- **writers**—people who write books or other items that can be read
- **writing**—the act of creating written words using various types of tools

Extension Idea

If possible, bring a laptop and typewriter for students to use. Allow them to type short sentences on both. Then, ask the students which was easier to use. Were there any advantages that one writing tool had over the other? Why might writers enjoy using a laptop more than a typewriter?

Write Away

Source: Photos.com

Today, a writer changes her work on a laptop computer.

Source: The Library of Congress

Typewriters were used by writers in the early 1900s.

Typing Away—An Echo Reading from the Past

Student 1

Writing tools have changed a lot over the years. The first writers did not have me to use. I am a typewriter. Instead, they had to draw pictures on rocks.

(audience echoes)

Student 2

The first writers used special sticks, too. These sticks were called styluses. The sticks could write on clay or wax.

(audience echoes)

Student 3

It is much easier to use me. All you have to do is put paper in me and press the keys. But, paper has changed, too. The first paper was called papyrus. This paper came from a plant in Egypt.

(audience echoes)

Student 4

My keys can get stuck. But, writers of long ago still had a much harder time. The first writers in America were called the Olmecs. They were American Indians. The Olmecs carved writing into clay or metal. Boy, talk about hard work!

(audience echoes)

Student 1

I came around in 1866. I had a keyboard that everyone could use.

(audience echoes)

Student 2

I made it easy to write. Writers could now use me to create their books. They no longer had to use pencils to write down their thoughts.

(audience echoes)

Student 3

I am so easy to use! Can I ever be replaced?

(audience echoes)

Typing Away—An Echo Reading from Today

Student 1

There are many tools we can use to write. I am a new tool that people use.

(audience echoes)

Student 2

Some people use pencils. Some use pens. But, a lot of people use me to write. I am a computer.

(audience echoes)

Student 3

There are a lot of ways that people use me. I am a laptop. I can be light and easy to carry.

(audience echoes)

Student 4

People can write a lot of things on me. Some people write letters and print them out. They can send the letters to their friends.

(audience echoes)

Student 1

Others use me to email their friends. Email means electronic mail. The mail is sent from one computer to another. It is a fast way to send mail.

(audience echoes)

Typing Away—An Echo
Reading from Today *(cont.)*

Student 2

You can keep a weblog on me, too. A weblog is a journal kept on the Internet. They can have pictures on them, too. Blogging can keep families in touch.

(audience echoes)

Student 3

Websites can be created on me. Websites are found on the Internet. They show pictures and news.

(audience echoes)

Student 4

I have a lot of uses. More and more uses are sure to come in the future!

(audience echoes)

Extra, Extra—Read All About It!

Objective

√ Students will perform a song for two voices fluently with changes in tone, volume, timing, and expression.

Materials/Preparation

- Create an overhead transparency of *Print Time* (page 94). Also, print copies of the primary source pictures for the students (filenames: writer03.jpg, writer04.jpg).
- Create an overhead transparency of *"Books, Wonderful Books"—A Song for Two Voices* (page 95). Also, make copies for the students.

Fluency Suggestions and Activities

You may want to complete the history and/or vocabulary activities on the following page before this fluency activity. An understanding of the historical context and vocabulary will help students analyze and read the piece fluently.

1. Divide the class into small groups. Give each group either a "then" or "now" primary source picture. Then, have the groups create charts on pieces of paper that are divided into three sections: *People*, *Places*, and *Things*. Ask each group to observe the photo given to them and write down the things they see that would fall under each of the three categories. Have the groups then share their charts with the class as you list their observations on the board. Display the transparency of *Print Time* (page 94) on the overhead. Compare the two pictures based on the groups' observations.

2. Place *"Books, Wonderful Books"—A Song for Two Voices* (page 95) on the overhead. Tell the class that they are going to read the song with partners. Read the song aloud to the class so that they can hear it at least once. Then, point out the lines in bold. Tell them that those lines are meant to be read together, with their partners. Then, the partners should take turns reading the other lines in regular type. "Voice 1" should be read by the first partner, and "Voice 2" by the second. Choose a volunteer to read the song with you. Read the song, with you being "Voice 1" and the volunteer being "Voice 2." Be sure to read the bolded words together. Model this once again, using a different volunteer.

3. Next, give the students their own copies of the song. Tell them that they are going to practice reading the song together, with partners, using proper tempo. Explain to them that tempo is the rate at which we read. We should not read too fast or too slow. Our tempos should make our reading smooth and easy to follow. Read the song using proper tempo. Then, read it too fast or too slow. Have the students compare the two readings to help them realize the importance of tempo.

4. Assign partners to students. Have them read the song with their partners, with one partner being "Voice 1" and the other partner being "Voice 2." Remind them to read the bolded verses together. Tell them that they will be performing the song for the music teacher. When they perform, they can either read or sing the song. Give students time to practice their songs. Then, invite the music teacher to your room. Choose two or three partner pairs to perform for the music teacher and the rest of the class.

Extra, Extra—Read All About It! *(cont.)*

History Connection

Many of the first books were published by monks. The monks from western Europe would copy books, such as the Bible, one at a time to be read by others. It wasn't until the 1400s that the printing press was invented, making the reproduction of books much easier. Johannes Gutenberg invented the printing press. Before the printing press, block printing was used. Block printing involved pressing sheets of paper into individually carved wooden blocks. This method is believed to have begun in China. Movable type was also invented in China in 1041. Though easier than block printing, each piece of movable type still had to be carved by hand. Gutenberg improved upon this by developing molds, which were easier to use than carving the letters by hand. The monks could take up to a year to hand copy the Bible. With Gutenberg's invention, several hundered copies of the Bible could be produced in a year.

Vocabulary Connection

Discuss unfamiliar vocabulary encountered in the text. Some possible words are listed below. After identifying the difficult words, discuss them within the context of the text.

- **adventure**—something exciting; thrill; risk
- **invented**—made up; devised; created for the first time
- **readable**—clear; easy to read
- **rhyme**—words that have the same ending sound

Extension Idea

To show students the tedious work of copying books by hand, ask them to rewrite the history connection in their best handwriting. Time how long, on average, it takes the students to copy the paragraph. Then, ask them how they would feel if they had to rewrite the same paragraph for every member of the class. What about for the entire school? Allow them to share their thoughts. You may also wish to share the history connection with students and create a class time line, showing the evolution of printing.

Print Time

Source: The Library of Congress

Monks copied books for others to read.

Source: Photos.com

The printing press makes copies of books and newspapers today.

"Books, Wonderful Books"— A Song for Two Voices

CHORUS—Both Voices

Beautiful, wonderful, readable books,

Oh, how I love your smell and looks!

I turn the page with joy and glee.

Who knows what adventure waits for me?

Voice 1

But, books, I wonder how you came to be.

Did you fall like a leaf straight from a tree?

Did you grow on a vine or drop from the sky

From the clutch of a hawk who was just flying by?

CHORUS—Both Voices

Voice 2

I'll find the answer! I know how to do it.

I'll find the right book and read right through it!

Look here! Yes, now I think I know.

The story goes back a long time ago.

CHORUS—Both Voices

Voice 1

Monks of old wrote each line themselves

Of every book that sat on the shelves.

Page by page they wrote each one

Until, at last, the whole book was done.

CHORUS—Both Voices

Voice 2

It took months to finish a book by pen,

And then they had to start again.

Until a man named Gutenberg

Changed the way to print each word.

CHORUS—Both Voices

Voice 1

He invented the amazing printing press,

And so the poor monks could take a rest!

Hundreds of books could print at one time!

And that, dear reader, is the end of this rhyme.

Getting Money

Objective

√ Students will read poems fluently with proper tone and volume using echo reading.

Materials/Preparation

- Create an overhead transparency of *Deposits and Withdrawals* (page 98). Also, print copies of the primary source pictures for the students (filenames: bank01.jpg, bank02.jpg).
- Create an overhead transparency of *"Two Ways to Bank"—An Echo Reading Poem* (page 99). Also, make copies for students.

Fluency Suggestions and Activities

You may want to complete the history and/or vocabulary activities on the following page before this fluency activity. An understanding of the historical context and vocabulary will help students analyze and read the piece fluently.

1. Divide the students into two groups. Give the first group the "then" picture of the antique bank counter. Give the second group the "now" picture of the ATM. Then, have the groups create three sentences to describe their pictures. Once the sentences are created, have the groups trade the photos and do the same with the other pictures. Ask volunteers to read their sentences aloud, first for the "then" picture and then for the "now" picture. Display the transparency of *Deposits and Withdrawals* (page 98) on the overhead. Ask the students how managing money has changed over the years. How have banks changed? Also ask them how the job of bank tellers has changed, due to having ATMs available to deposit and withdraw money. You may wish to discuss with them what ATM means and how it relates to bank tellers. Write the students' answers to the questions on the board.

2. Place the transparency of *"Two Ways to Bank"—An Echo Reading Poem* (page 99) on the overhead. Read the poem aloud to the students. Model the use of flow and pace as you read. First, read the poem with smoothness, adding attention to expression. Then, read the poem in a monotone voice. Ask the students which reading was better. Explain how to use proper phrasing and flow when reading.

3. Next, give the students their own copies of the poem. Tell them that they are now going to practice reading in groups of five. Their small groups will later perform for bank tellers in the community. Before having the groups practice, explain how to perform an echo reading by asking volunteers to echo what you read. Assign the volunteers the student parts, and model the echo reading for the rest of the class. Then, place the students into their small groups.

4. Have students practice their readings in their small groups. Ask them to circle any unknown words as they read, making sure they practice those words. This way, they can make sure their reading flows and has correct pacing. Allow students time to practice their echo readings.

5. Invite bank tellers from the community to the classroom to discuss working at banks with the class. Then, assign each bank teller a group and allow the groups to perform their poems for the bank tellers, or allow the entire class to perform in one large echo reading.

Getting Money *(cont.)*

History Connection

The way we get money from banks has changed throughout the years. Long ago, passbooks were kept to show the money deposited or withdrawn from accounts. Bank tellers would sign these passbooks as transactions were made. Today, computers keep track of accounts. With the invention of the ATM, or automated teller machine, getting money has become easier and more convenient. Although the first ATM was patented in 1939 by Luther George Simjian, this machine was not successful. The first working ATM was installed in the New York based Chemical Bank after Don Wetzel invented his successful and modern ATM in 1968. Since then, ATMs have been connected to bank accounts and computers around the world, making banking easier for customers.

Vocabulary Connection

Discuss unfamiliar vocabulary encountered in the text. Some possible words are listed below. After identifying the difficult words, discuss them within the context of the text.

- **deposit**—putting money into a bank account
- **loan**—money given to someone to borrow
- **PIN**—personal identification number
- **stellar**—outstanding; the best
- **withdrawal**—taking money out of a bank account

Extension Idea

Create passbooks for students by folding small sheets of paper and stapling them together. Give each student an account with a certain dollar amount listed. Then, give the students opportunities to earn classroom money throughout the week. Students may earn money for appropriate behavior or helping around the classroom. Allow students to deposit their money into your bank as they earn it. Also allow them to withdraw their money to spend at a classroom store. Ask students to keep track of their withdrawals and deposits. Then, at the end of the week, ask the students if it was easy to keep records of their banking transactions. Would it have been easier for bank tellers or ATMs to do it for them? Discuss the pros and cons of both the ATMs and passbooks.

Deposits and Withdrawals

Source: iStockphoto.com/Richard Walters

This is an old bank counter. Tellers stood behind it
and helped the customers with their money.

Source: Scott/BigStockPhoto.com

Today, a bank customer uses an ATM.
The machine lets her withdraw money from her account.

"Two Ways to Bank"— An Echo Reading Poem

Student 1

Money out, money in,

Press the buttons to begin.

Making a withdrawal or deposit?

Just use your card and PIN to cause it.

(audience echoes)

Student 2

The ATM is fast and easy.

It makes banking quick and breezy.

But for service, it's not stellar.

For that you need a banking teller.

(audience echoes)

Student 3

The teller smiles and says hello.

Got a question? She will know.

She'll cash a check or count the cash.

Need a loan? She'll get it fast.

(audience echoes)

Student 4

Only a teller can think and read

And help with all your money needs.

For the teller, the machine's a perk,

But the ATM needs the teller to work.

(audience echoes)

Student 5

An ATM sure is handy,

And for speedy banking, it's dandy.

But for the best service just for you,

The teller's the one to see it through.

(audience echoes)

Safe Keeping

Objective

√ Students will read passages fluently and accurately within a choral-reading activity, focusing on volume and expressive language.

Materials/Preparation

- Create an overhead transparency of *Behind Bars* (page 102). If preferred, print copies of the primary source pictures for the students (filenames: bank03.jpg, bank04.jpg).
- Create an overhead transparency of *Inside the Vault—A Choral Reading* (page 103). Also, make copies for the students.

Fluency Suggestions and Activities

You may want to complete the history and/or vocabulary activities on the following page before this fluency activity. An understanding of the historical context and vocabulary will help students analyze and read the piece fluently.

1. Divide the class into three groups. Ask the class to brainstorm lists of places used to keep things safe. Have the groups share their lists with the class. Then, place *Behind Bars* (page 102) on the overhead. Have the groups list adjectives to describe the "then" picture. Ask them to do the same for the "now" picture. Compare the two lists. Did the groups use any of the same words to describe both vaults? How were the vaults different?

2. Place *Inside the Vault—A Choral Reading* (page 103) on the overhead. Prior to class, tape-record the reading. Then, play the tape-recording of the reading with the class, as you read along with it, in a choral reading. Tell the class that choral reading is when a group of students read the same text aloud together. Explain that you did a choral reading along with the tape recorder, and they will be doing choral readings in small groups.

3. Before having students practice their choral reading, tell them that using voice helps the reading come alive. Play the recording of the reading again. Then, ask the students what type of voice was used in the reading. Was it a scary voice? A friendly voice? Allow them to describe the voice used in the reading. Discuss the types of voices appropriate for the reading. How would the reading sound if it were read in a scary voice? Would that show the meaning of the reading? Explain the importance of using proper voice when reading.

4. Give each student a copy of the reading. Reread it together in a choral reading. Have the class use proper voice as they read.

5. Place students into small groups and have them practice using choral readings within their groups. Allow the class to practice their choral readings in their small groups until they become comfortable enough to perform the reading.

6. Allow each group to perform the reading in front of the class. Have the class choose the group that did the best. That group can recite the reading for another class.

Safe Keeping *(cont.)*

History Connection

Bank vaults usually contain safe deposit boxes, cash drawers, and valuable assets of the bank or its customers. Bank vaults are made of thick steel and concrete. They have alarms that can be set off if a lot of noise is made over a long period of time. This helps to deter any robbers. Time locks have also been used on vaults since 1874. This allows the vaults to only be opened using combinations at particular times of the day.

Vocabulary Connection

Discuss unfamiliar vocabulary encountered in the text. Some possible words are listed below. After identifying the difficult words, discuss them within the context of the text.

- **combination**—a series of numbers used to open a lock
- **customer**—someone who pays for a product or service
- **important**—of great value
- **safe deposit boxes**—metal fireproof boxes that store valuable items
- **valuables**—things that are treasured

Extension Idea

Ask students to pretend they are architects who have been asked to design new bank vaults. How would they look? What building materials would they use? How would they keep valuables safe? Then, have them draw pictures of their vaults, as well as what contents or valuables of their own they would keep inside their vaults.

Behind Bars

Source: The Library of Congress

A bank vault is built behind steel bars. Money is kept inside the vault.

Source: iStockphoto.com/Robert Kyllo

The large vault door keeps money and other valuables safe.

Inside the Vault—A Choral Reading

Hello! We are glad to have you at First Bank. I am a bank teller here. Today, we are going to take a tour of the bank's vault.

A bank's vault keeps customers' money safe. We keep the bank's money in it, too.

You can find safe deposit boxes in a vault. Customers keep valuables in these boxes. They may also keep important papers in them. This way, their items are kept safe.

Our vaults have large doors made of steel and concrete. A bank vault time lock is on the vault. The door stays locked until the timer runs down. When the timer goes off, the door can be opened.

But, a combination has to be used to open the door. We use a timer to keep the vault locked. The door cannot be opened at night. This helps us keep bank robbers away!

Bank vaults have not changed a lot over the years. They still have timer locks. And, they still keep our customers' valuables nice and safe!

Checking Out

Objective

√ Students will improve expressive reading skills by engaging in reader's theater.

Materials/Preparation

- Create an overhead transparency for *Ringing Up the Sales* (page 106). If preferred, print copies of the primary source pictures for the students (filename: store01.jpg, store02.jpg).
- Copy *In the Checkout Line—Reader's Theater* (pages 107–109) for each student.
- Make copies of the *Expression Prereading Sheet* (page 110) and *Expression Evaluation* (page 111) for each student.

Fluency Suggestions and Activities

You may want to complete the history and/or vocabulary activities on the following page before this fluency activity. An understanding of the historical context and vocabulary will help students analyze and read the piece fluently.

1. Place the transparency of *Ringing Up the Sales* (page 106) on the overhead. Ask the students how we buy our groceries at the store. How has buying groceries changed? How is the store clerk in the "then" photo helping the customer? What tools are being used? What tools are used in the "now" photo? How has the technology changed? Does it make purchasing items at a store easier? Ask students to list the pros and cons of purchasing items in each of the photographs. Then, take a class vote to decide on which way is the easiest—then or now?

2. Write each of the following expressions on a separate sheet of paper: *frightened, surprised, excited, sad,* and *angry.* Ask five volunteers to each choose one piece of paper. Then, have the volunteers read, "There's the store," using the expression written on their papers.

3. After the volunteers have read their sentences using the various expressions, ask the class how expressions can change the meaning of a sentence. Tell them that the use of expression makes reading come alive. It shows the feelings of the reader. Explain to them that it is very important to use the proper expressions when performing a reading.

4. Give each student a copy of *In the Checkout Line—Reader's Theater* (pages 107–109). Read the script together first as a class, choosing six students to read the parts. Then, allow students to choose the parts they wish to perform, or assign them their parts. Since there are six parts, you may choose to assign only six students the parts. If time permits, you may choose to assign every student a part and allow time for several performances.

5. Distribute a copy of *Expression Prereading Sheet* (page 110) to each student. Review the directions with the students, and have them complete their sheets before their performances.

6. Place students in small groups. Allow them to practice with their group members, paying special attention to expression. Once students are comfortable performing their scripts, allow them to perform for other teachers or the principal. After the performances, have each student complete *Expression Evaluation* (page 111).

Checking Out (cont.)

History Connection

Before barcode scanners, store clerks took inventory manually. Store clerks would count every item in the store. Then, in the nineteenth century, the punch card technique was introduced. The idea was for customers to punch cards to mark their selections. At the checkout counter, the cards would be put in a reader so that the inventory could be counted. However, this technique was not very popular.

The idea of the modern barcode was invented in 1948 by Norman Woodland, who used Morse Code, or a series of dots and dashes, in his invention. But it wasn't until 1972 that the first scanner was installed and used in a Cincinnati Kroger store. The scanner read the barcodes of the products. It proved to be a faster and more efficient way to check out.

Vocabulary Connection

Discuss unfamiliar vocabulary encountered in the text. Some possible words are listed below. After identifying the difficult words, discuss them within the context of the text.

- **cash register**—a tool used to add up bills and store money
- **computers**—tools that can store data and find information on the Internet
- **conveyer belt**—a moving belt that can transport or move objects
- **general store**—a store that has a variety of products or items for sale
- **groceries**—food items
- **inventory**—a list of all the items available or in stock
- **manager**—the person in charge
- **mistakes**—errors; items that are not correct
- **scanner**—a tool that scans an item, putting the information from the item onto a computer

Extension Idea

Have a cash register and hand-written ticket relay in your classroom. Divide the class into two teams—the cash register team and the hand-written ticket team. Prior to the activity, ask the students to bring in boxes and cans of food items. Also, bring a toy cash register to class. Then, assign two students to be the store clerks. The other students will be the shoppers. Ask the students to go shopping for two items each, and then stand in their assigned lines. Have the store clerks check out their shoppers. You may also wish to give the shoppers pretend money to use to pay the store clerks. Once the last shopper has paid for his/her goods, ask the students which line moved faster. Why? How has technology made it easier and faster to shop?

Ringing Up the Sales

Source: The Library of Congress

A store clerk writes a grocery bill for a customer. The year is 1948.

Source: Photos.com

Today, this store clerk uses a computer and a scanner to ring up customers.

In the Checkout Line— Reader's Theater

Characters

Joey, an eight-year-old boy   Hannah, a seven-year-old girl
Grandpa Jesse   Grandma Audrey
Store Clerk Stan   Manager Marie

Hannah: One dollar and fifty cents. I have just enough money to buy a pack of gum!

Grandpa Jesse: Wow! A pack of gum costs that much money?

Grandma Audrey: In our day, we only had to pay five cents.

Joey: Five cents! Oh, man! I could save money for gum if it was only five cents!

Grandpa Jesse: Put your gum on the conveyer belt so the store clerk can scan it.

Grandma Audrey: Boy, Grandpa! Did you ever think you would be using words like *conveyer belt* and *scanner*?

Hannah: What do you mean, Grandma?

Grandma Audrey: When we used to go to the general store, Mr. Henderson would write up our bill. Then, he would add up the total on paper.

Grandpa Jesse: That was until he got that fancy new cash register.

Store Clerk Stan: Your total is two dollars, please.

Hannah: Two dollars? How could that be? The price says it is only one dollar and fifty cents.

In the Checkout Line— Reader's Theater *(cont.)*

Store Clerk Stan: Hmmm! Let me see.

Joey: It looks like it rang up wrong on the computer.

Store Clerk Stan: Let me call the manager. She'll know what to do.

Grandpa Jesse: I must say, computers sure are nice. But, Mr. Henderson never wrote down the wrong price!

Joey: You mean, he wrote down every item you bought?

Grandma Audrey: Yep! Then, he added them all up. Boy, could he add!

Hannah: Do you think he was faster than a scanner, Grandma?

Grandma Audrey: Well, I don't know about that! But, he did not make many mistakes.

Manager Marie: How can I help you all?

Store Clerk Stan: The computer is showing the wrong price for this pack of gum.

Manager Marie: Computers are nice and fast. But, they can still make mistakes. You're right. The gum doesn't cost two dollars. Let me just fix this real fast on the computer.

Hannah: If computers make mistakes, why do we use them?

Store Clerk Stan: Well, the computers are right most of the time.

Manager Marie: Plus, they can add the long lists of groceries quickly.

In the Checkout Line— Reader's Theater *(cont.)*

Grandma Audrey: And, they keep inventory of what is in the store.

Joey: Inventory? What's that?

Grandpa Jesse: Stores have to know what products they have. That way, they can make sure they have enough items for all of their customers.

Grandma Audrey: That's right. Before scanners, store clerks had to count all of the groceries in the store. That was the only way they could tell how many of each item they had.

Grandpa Jesse: That took a long time!

Manager Marie: Thanks to scanners, our computers can keep track of our products.

Store Clerk Stan: But, store clerks are still here to make sure that no mistakes are made, like with your gum.

Grandpa Jesse: Today, checking out at the store is much easier for customers and store clerks.

Hannah: Yeah, I guess you're right, Grandpa! As long as I do not have to pay two dollars for my pack of gum!

Expression Prereading Sheet

Name: _____

Directions: Look through your lines from the script. Then, decide which expressions you should use when reading those lines. Write your lines. List the expressions you'll use under them. Then, practice your lines. Be sure to use those expressions.

Section One

   1. Line One: _____

     _____

     Expression to Use: _____

   2. Line Two: _____

     _____

     Expression to Use: _____

   3. Line Three: _____

     _____

     Expression to Use: _____

   4. Line Four: _____

     _____

     Expression to Use: _____

   5. Line Five: _____

     _____

     Expression to Use:_____

Expression Evaluation

Name: _____

Directions: Think about your performance. Did you use the correct expressions in your performance? Answer the questions below about the expressions you used.

1. Line One Expression: _____

   Did I use the expression in my performance?   Yes   No

2. Line Two Expression: _____

   Did I use the expression in my performance?   Yes   No

3. Line Three Expression: _____

   Did I use the expression in my performance?   Yes   No

4. Line Four Expression: _____

   Did I use the expression in my performance?   Yes   No

5. Line Five Expression: _____

   Did I use the expression in my performance?   Yes   No

6. How can I make my performance better? _____

   _____

   _____

7. What other expressions can I use? _____

   _____

8. The thing I liked best about my performance is: _____

   _____

9. I liked using the _____ expression best because

   _____ .

Shopping Day

Objective

√ Students will read passages fluently and accurately within a paired-reading activity.

Materials/Preparation

- Create an overhead transparency of *Shop 'Til You Drop* (page 114). If preferred, print copies of the primary source pictures for the students (filenames: store03.jpg, store04.jpg).
- Create an overhead transparency of *Searching for Store Clerks—Paired Reading* (pages 115–116). Also, make copies for the students.

Fluency Suggestions and Activities

You may want to complete the history and/or vocabulary activities on the following page before this fluency activity. An understanding of the historical context and vocabulary will help students analyze and read the piece fluently.

1. Give each student a blank sheet of paper. Have the students draw their favorite stores on their papers. What do those stores sell? How do they look? Then, place *Shop 'Til You Drop* (page 114) on the overhead. Ask the students to list everything they see in the "then" picture of the general store. Write the items the students list on the board. Do the same with the "now" mall picture. Discuss how we shop for items today (with specialized stores) compared to general stores of the past. Then, have students compare their drawings to the two photos. How are the items sold? Are the layouts of the stores the same? How are they different?

2. Next, place *Searching for Store Clerks—Paired Reading* (pages 115–116) on the overhead. Read the first ad aloud. As you read, focus on reading the letter smoothly. Do this again with the second ad. Then, read the two ads again, but this time, sound out words and stumble over some of the reading. Also repeat words and take long pauses. Ask the class how the second reading sounded. Was it easy to understand? What could you do to make the reading better? Explain the importance of reading smoothly.

3. Next, ask a volunteer to read the ads with you. Read the ads together with the volunteer in a paired reading. Tell the students that they will be reading the ads together in paired readings. They can read the ads chorally with their partners, or they can take turns with their partners reading every other line. Explain to the students that they will be performing the ads with their partners for the rest of the class. Then, the class will vote on three partner pairs to read the ads over the intercom.

4. Give each student a copy of the two want ads. Place them with partners. Have the students practice paired readings, focusing on reading smoothly.

5. Once the groups have practiced, allow them to perform the paired reading for the class. Then, have the class vote on three groups that will perform over the intercom. Set up a time for the groups to perform.

Shopping Day *(cont.)*

History Connection

General stores were commonly found in small towns or rural areas. These stores contained a wide selection of merchandise to be sold. Items ranging from food to household and electrical supplies could be found at the general stores. In the first half of the twentieth century, general stores began to be replaced by specialized retailers. Few general stores still exist today. However, the convenience of the general store can still be seen in modern stores, such as the convenience store.

Malls have existed for more than 1,000 years, with people shopping at bazaars, or large covered shopping areas. These covered specialized stores were introduced in the United States in the 1800s, but did not gain popularity until the early 1900s.

Vocabulary Connection

Discuss unfamiliar vocabulary encountered in the text. Some possible words are listed below. After identifying the difficult words, discuss them within the context of the text.

- **cash register**—a tool used to add up bills and store money
- **credit cards**—cards people use to buy items and make payments later
- **customers**—people who pay for products or services
- **general store**—a store that has a variety of products or items for sale
- **holidays**—customs; festivals; celebrations; vacations
- **inventory**—a list of all of the items available or in stock
- **machines**—devices used to assist people
- **merchandise**—items for sale
- **payments**—paying money at a store in order to get items in return
- **return**—to bring back an item to the store

Extension Idea

Have each student create two sales ads: a "then" sales ad and a "now" sales ad. Their ads should show pictures of items found in the stores from the "then" photo and items we find in stores today, as well as prices for those items. You may wish to find price listings for prices "then" and "now" on the Internet for students to use in their ads.

Shop 'Til You Drop

Source: The Library of Congress

Items such as soap and dishes are stacked on the shelves of this general store in 1936.

Source: Photos.com

Shoppers find everything from jewelry to clothes at a modern mall.

Searching for Store Clerks— Paired Reading

Date: 1854

Wanted—Store Clerk

Job Description:

The general store on Main Street is looking for a friendly face. As the store clerk, you will be asked to stock the shelves with our new merchandise. The items will need price tags, too. You will need to take inventory of our merchandise as well. We are the only store in town where our customers can shop. So, we can never run out of items. You will be writing up customers' bills. You will ring up their items on our cash register, too. As our store clerk, you will have to count money and take payments from the customers.

Schooling Needed:

No schooling is needed.

Skills Needed:

Some math skills are needed. And, you must be a kind person who likes to help others.

Searching for Store Clerks—
Paired Reading *(cont.)*

Date: Present Day

Wanted—Sales Clerk

Job Description:

Do you like clothes? Or maybe toys? Then the job at the Springfield Mall is the place for you! Store clerks are needed for the holidays. It is our busiest time of year. You can choose the retail shop for which you wish to work. And, there are a lot of shops to choose from in our mall! As a store clerk, you will be asked to scan merchandise. You will take payments, too. Our customers will want you to help them find the items they need. You will need to help stock shelves. You will also have to put price tags on new items. As a store clerk, you will be using credit card machines and cash registers. You will need to help our customers when they have items to return.

Schooling Needed:

No schooling is needed.

Skills Needed:

Math skills are needed. And, you must be a kind person who likes to help others.

The Catch of the Day

Objective

√ Students will practice divided reading of a text in preparation for a performance.

Materials/Preparation

- Create an overhead transparency of *Fishing Around* (page 119). If preferred, print copies of the primary source pictures for the students (filenames: fisher01.jpg, fisher02.jpg).
- Create an overhead transparency of *"Fishing Yesterday and Today"—Divided Reading* (page 120). Also, make copies for the students.
- Copy *Flow Practice and Evaluation* (page 121) for each student.

Fluency Suggestions and Activities

You may want to complete the history and/or vocabulary activities on the following page before this fluency activity. An understanding of the historical context and vocabulary will help students analyze and read the piece fluently.

1. Display the transparency of *Fishing Around* (page 119) on the overhead. Only show the "then" picture. Place the students into small groups. Have the groups describe the picture using three to five sentences. Allow them to share their descriptions. Then, do the same with the "now" picture. Ask the students if their "then" and "now" descriptions had any similarities. How were they different? Ask them how fishing, one of the world's first jobs, has changed. How has it stayed the same?

2. Place the transparency of *"Fishing Yesterday and Today"—Divided Reading* (page 120) on the overhead. Then, read the song aloud to the students. Explain that as the song is practiced, flow will improve, and the text will be more understandable. Model fluent reading, especially the use of flow, as you read the song once again to the students.

3. Explain to the students that the song has been divided into parts. Distribute copies of the song to the students. Have students read the song silently, searching for unfamiliar words. Ask them to underline those words in the text. Then, give each student a copy of *Flow Practice and Evaluation* (page 121). Review the directions with students. Have them complete the first section.

4. Divide the class into four different groups. Assign each group a number. Tell the groups these numbers will represent the stanzas they will read from the song. Tell the students they should read their assigned parts with their groups until they are comfortable reading their parts aloud to the class. Have them concentrate on flow, making sure that they do not stumble over any words. Once they are comfortable reading their parts aloud, have the groups perform the divided reading as a class. You may vote as a class whether to sing the text or simply read it.

5. Invite parents to your room. Have the class perform the divided reading for the parents. You may want to have the students practice first by performing for another class.

6. The students should then complete the second and third portions of the *Flow Practice and Evaluation* sheet after their performances.

The Catch of the Day *(cont.)*

History Connection

The earliest fishers used knives or spears to catch fish. Later, fishing lines, hooks, and nets were used. In early days, the fishers would stand in shallow water to catch fish. This limited the type of fish that could be caught. But, once boats were used, fishers could catch larger fish. Boats with sails were the first types of boats used in the fishing industry. Soon, steamships and then motorboats took their place. With the development of motorboats, fishers could go further out to sea and stay for longer periods of time.

Computers are now also found in boats. These computers tell the captains where the best fishing spots are. However, staying out to sea for longer periods has made fishing a dangerous job. The ocean's unpredictable weather causes many fishing injuries and deaths.

With fishing tools becoming more developed, some fish have also become endangered. Due to this, laws have been created to keep the fish from becoming extinct.

Vocabulary Connection

Discuss unfamiliar vocabulary encountered in the text. Some possible words are listed below. After identifying the difficult words, discuss them within the context of the text.

- **spear**—a long rod with a sharp end used to catch fish
- **steady**—stable; not easily moved

Extension Idea

Divide the class into two groups—fishers today and fishers from long ago. Tell the students to pretend to be fishers from their assigned groups. They have just come back from a day of fishing. What did they experience? What tools did they use? How many fish did they catch? What was their day like? Have them use the "then" and "now" photos, the "Fishing Yesterday and Today" song, and the History Connection to create diary entries about their day. Or, they may choose to dress up as the "then" or "now" fishers and create fishing tools out of simple art supplies. They may then orally tell about their days to the class, rather than writing diary entries.

Fishing Around

Source: Photos.com

Fishers use modern motorboats to find large fish.

Source: The Library of Congress

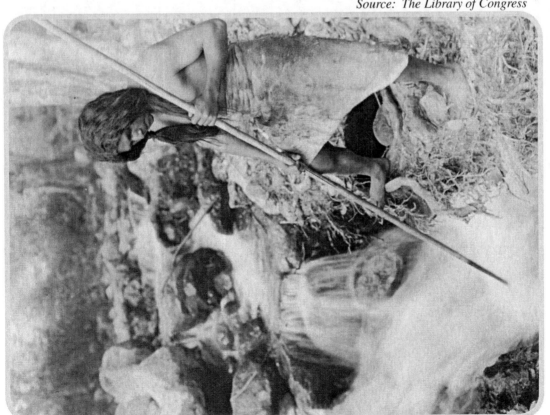

A Hupa Indian stands near a stream.
He hopes to catch salmon with his spear.

"Fishing Yesterday and Today"— Divided Reading

Group 1

Oh, to the water,

To the water I go,

My spear in hand,

My boat to row.

Group 2

The water rushes.

I head to the calm.

My aim is steady.

My net is strong.

Group 3

I look to the river.

I look to the sea.

I have only myself.

My partner's with me.

Group 4

I spy my fish.

The whole school I'll get.

I raise my spear.

I throw my net.

Group 1

I catch my fish!

I make my haul.

Now home I turn

Before nightfall.

Flow Practice and Evaluation

Name: _____

Directions: Write the words from the song that you need to practice reading fluently in section one. Practice the words. Then, perform the song. Write any words you still need to practice in section two. Keep practicing the words. Perform the song again until you can read all the words fluently.

Section One

Words to practice:

1. _____

2. _____

3. _____

4. _____

Section Two

Words I missed:

1. _____

2. _____

3. _____

4. _____

Section Three

Ways I improved on my last performance:

My reading was smooth and flowed well. Yes or No

What I liked best about my reading: _____

_____

What I would change about my reading: _____

_____

A Day at the Fish Market

Objective

√ Students will read a passage fluently and accurately using the call-and-response method.

Materials/Preparation

- Create an overhead transparency of *The Fish Market* (page 124). If preferred, print copies of the primary source pictures for the students (filenames: fisher03.jpg, fisher04.jpg).
- Create an overhead transparency of *Fish for Sale—Call and Response Ad* (page 125). Also, make copies for the students.

Fluency Suggestions and Activities

You may want to complete the history and/or vocabulary activities on the following page before this fluency activity. An understanding of the historical context and vocabulary will help students analyze and read the piece fluently.

1. Place the transparency of *The Fish Market* (page 124) on the overhead. Ask the students to carefully look at the "then" photo. Ask them the following questions: *What are the people doing? What are they selling? Where are the fish that are being sold?* Do the same with the "now" picture. Then, ask the students to write new captions for both pictures. Their captions should tell what is going on in the photos. Allow them to share their captions with the class.

2. Display the transparency of *Fish for Sale—Call and Response Ad* (page 125). Read the ad aloud to the students. Model fluent reading, especially the use of tempo, as you read. Explain to the class that when reading, they should use the same pace. Their readings should neither be too fast nor too slow.

3. Give each student a copy of the ad. Reread the entire text chorally, as a class. Practice the reading several times. Then, tell students that you need volunteers to read the various parts of the ad. But, the entire class will read the lines that are bolded. Have the class practice the call and response several times. Then, ask them if using proper tempo is easier when reading chorally with the class. Tell the students to concentrate on using proper pace and tempo as they read.

4. Place students into groups of six. Assign the members of the groups the various parts to read. Remind them to use correct tempo as they read. Allow the class to practice their call-and-response choral readings in their small groups until they become comfortable enough to perform the reading. You may also remind them to use proper expressions in their readings to make the ad come alive.

5. Tell the students that they will be filmed while performing the reading. These films will be used as commercials for the ad. Then, students will watch the videotape as a class.

A Day at the Fish Market (cont.)

History Connection

As the fishing industry grew, better tools were developed. With these better tools and larger boats, more fish were being caught than could be eaten in a day. Fishers soon had to find ways to preserve the fish before selling them at the market. Before the use of refrigeration, fish were dried, salted, or smoked to keep them from spoiling. Today, fishing boats have holds on them to help keep the fish cold. This allows them to stay out at sea for longer periods of time.

Vocabulary Connection

Discuss unfamiliar vocabulary encountered in the text. Some possible words are listed below. After identifying the difficult words, discuss them within the context of the text.

- **drying**—taking the water out of something wet
- **grouper**—a type of fish that lives at the bottom of the ocean
- **market**—a place where goods are bought
- **red snapper**—a type of fish that is red and is found in the ocean
- **salting**—adding salt to food to keep something from going bad
- **smoking**—adding smoke to food for flavor

Extension Idea

Give each student a large sheet of blank paper. Tell them that they are advertisers for the local fish market. They have been asked to create billboards that would make people want to buy the fresh fish. What would they put on their billboards? How would they make people want to visit the fish market? Have them create their billboards using the photos and the *"Fish for Sale"—Call and Response Ad* as inspiration.

The Fish Market

Source: The Library of Congress

Fresh fish lay on the tables. The people
decide what they want to buy. The year is 1890.

Source: iStockphoto.com/Daniel Tang

Fresh fish are put on ice. The fish is sold to customers today.

Fish for Sale—Call and Response Ad

All: **Fish for sale! Fresh fish for sale!**

R1: Visit the Fresh Catch Fish Market. You'll be hooked once you try our fresh fish. The fishers have just brought them in from the sea!

All: **Fish for sale! Fresh fish for sale!**

R2: They keep them in their holds. The holds are in the boats. It keeps the fish fresh until the fishers can get them to the market. No more smoking, drying, or salting the fish like we used to do. Just fresh fish waiting for you!

All: **Fish for sale! Fresh fish for sale!**

R3: We have all types of fish! There is red snapper, crab, shrimp, grouper, and more! We know you'll find something you like!

All: **Fish for sale! Fresh fish for sale!**

R4: We keep our fish nice and cold! We do this by laying them on ice!

All: **Fish for sale! Fresh fish for sale!**

R5: So, come visit us! Take a look around and choose the fish that is right for you!

All: **Fish for sale! Fresh fish for sale!**

R6: Our fish market is the best! Once we reel you in, you'll be hooked!

The Cleaning Crew

Objective

√ Students will read a poem fluently and accurately within a cumulative choral-reading activity, focusing on voice and expressive language.

Materials/Preparation

- Create an overhead transparency of *Taking Away the Trash* (page 128). If preferred, print copies of the primary source pictures for students (filenames: santtn01.jpg, santtn02.jpg).
- Create an overhead transparency of *Trash Pickup—Cumulative Choral Reading* (pages 129–130). Also, make copies for the students.

Fluency Suggestions and Activities

You may want to complete the history and/or vocabulary activities on the following page before this fluency activity. An understanding of the historical context and vocabulary will help students analyze and read the piece fluently.

1. Give each student a blank sheet of paper. Ask the students to draw pictures of the garbage trucks they see in the community. Allow them to share their pictures in small groups. Then, place the transparency of *Taking Away the Trash* (page 128) on the overhead. Show students the "then" photo of the garbage being collected by a sled on the overhead. Ask students how their pictures are similar to the photo. How are their pictures different from the photo? Do the same with the "now" photograph of the modern day garbage truck.

2. Place the transparency of *Trash Pickup—Cumulative Choral Reading* (pages 129–130) on the overhead. Read the cumulative choral reading aloud. As you read, focus on the use of voice to show your emotions. Then, read the page in a monotone voice. Ask the class which reading sounded best. Explain the importance of using voice to show feelings and emotions when reading. Also explain the content of the page and why trash pickup is so important to the community.

3. Next, explain to the students that they are going to practice reading the page in a cumulative choral reading. They will be placed in groups of four, and each member will be assigned a number. Explain that R1, R2, R3, and R4 mean Readers One, Two, Three, and Four. The first reader will begin reading. The next reader will then read with him or her, and this will continue until the entire group is reading the text together. Then, one by one, readers will stop reading, until only the first reader is left reading the passage. Demonstrate this process with volunteers using sentences from the reading.

4. Give each student a copy of the choral reading. Divide the students into groups and assign them numbers. Have the students practice their cumulative choral readings, focusing on the use of voice. Tell them that one group will be performing the reading for the principal. Therefore, the group that uses the best voice will be asked to perform.

5. Invite the principal to your room. Allow the group that used the best emotion and voice to perform for the principal. You may choose the group, or you may have the class vote.

The Cleaning Crew *(cont.)*

History Connection

Waste management is the business of getting rid of waste. If garbage is not managed and taken away in a sanitary way, it can spread disease. Pigs were once used to control waste. They were sent to garbage dumps to eat the trash. But, the pigs got very sick. Then, burning dumps were created to burn the trash. But, this caused air pollution. In the 1940s, landfills began to be used. These large areas of land were often lined with clay or plastic to keep the rats and insects away, as well as to keep garbage from seeping into the earth. These landfills are still used today.

In the early 1900s, garbage was carried away in carts pulled by hand or by horses. Heavy loads had to be lifted into the carts, which made this job quite difficult. Later, large trucks were used to pick up and move the waste. In the 1950s, equipment such as trash compactors were added to the trucks. These trash compactors pressed down the trash, allowing for more room in the trucks. Now, hydraulic lifts are also found on trucks. These help sanitation workers lift the trash into the back of the trucks.

Vocabulary Connection

Discuss unfamiliar vocabulary encountered in the text. Some possible words are listed below. After identifying the difficult words, discuss them within the context of the text.

- **equipment**—tools used to do a job
- **garbage**—waste; trash
- **hydraulic lift**—a bed of a truck that is lifted by a motor
- **landfills**—places where waste and trash are taken to be buried
- **sanitation workers**—people whose job is to make towns and cities clean by picking up trash and getting rid of waste
- **trash compactor**—a machine that presses down waste

Extension Idea

Ask the students to think about what our world would look like if we had no sanitation workers to pick up our trash. Then, to help them realize the amount of trash taken away by the sanitation workers, ask the students to place trash items that are nonperishable and not messy into a special bin for a week. Have the students then create a class mural, gluing all of the trash onto a large sheet of butcher paper. Ask the students to think about how much trash would be glued to the paper if the entire school would have saved their trash for a week. What if trash was saved for the entire year? Allow students to express the importance of having sanitation workers in our community.

Taking Away the Trash

Source: The Library of Congress

A horse pulls garbage on a sled. The year is 1939.

Source: Photos.com

A modern garbage truck empties trash. It is placed in a landfill.

Trash Pickup—Cumulative Choral Reading

R1: Our world has a lot of trash. We need people to help us get rid of all of our garbage. These people are called sanitation workers. But, being a sanitation worker is not easy.

R1, R2: Picking up trash has changed a lot. Today, trucks are used to pick up trash. But, before that, pigs were used. These pigs ate the garbage in the street.

R1, R2, R3: They did not do a very good job, though. The streets began to smell. So, pigs were no longer used.

R1, R2, R3, R4: **Then, garbage was taken away in carts or sleds. These carts were pulled by hand or by horses. This was not an easy job! The heavy trash had to be lifted into the carts. It was hard work!**

R1, R2, R3: Finally, trucks were used. These trucks took the trash to landfills.

R1, R2: The landfills were large areas of land. The land was lined with clay or plastic. This protected the earth from the garbage.

R1: But, sanitation workers still had to lift the trash into the trucks. Luckily, they did not have to unload the trash. Dump trucks were used for that. They could tilt back and dump the trash into the landfills.

R1, R2: Now, even more equipment has been added to the garbage trucks.

Trash Pickup—Cumulative Choral Reading *(cont.)*

R1, R2, R3: Today, trash compactors are put on trucks. They press down the garbage. This makes more room for other trash to be added.

R1, R2, R3, R4: Hydraulic lifts have been added, too.

R1, R2, R3: These lifts help sanitation workers. The lifts pick up the trash and put it into the back of the trucks.

R1, R2: The lifts make the job of the sanitation worker a little easier.

R1: Sanitation workers deserve all of the help they can get! Without them, our world would not be a clean place to live.

Swept Away

Objective

√ Students will deliver a group presentation and read passages fluently with proper tone and volume using echo reading.

Materials/Preparation

- Create an overhead transparency of *Sweeping Changes* (page 133). Also, print copies of the primary source pictures for students (filenames: santtn03.jpg, santtn04.jpg).
- Create overhead transparencies of *Street Sweeping Letter from the Past—Echo Reading* (page 134) and *Street Sweeping Letter from Today—Echo Reading* (page 135). Also, make copies for the students.
- Copy *Fluency Evaluation* (page 136) for each student.

Fluency Suggestions and Activities

You may want to complete the history and/or vocabulary activities on the following page before this fluency activity. An understanding of the historical context and vocabulary will help students analyze and read the piece fluently.

1. Place students into two groups. Give one group the "then" photo of the sanitation worker sweeping the streets and the other group the "now" photo. Ask the groups to pretend to be sanitation workers in the photos, either sweeping the streets with a broom or driving the street sweeper. Have the groups write three sentences to describe the sanitation workers' day based on the photos. Then, allow them to read their descriptions aloud. Discuss how the descriptions were similar and different. Then, show the class both pictures using the transparency of *Sweeping Changes* (page 133) on the overhead. Discuss other similarities and differences with the class.

2. Place the transparencies of *Street Sweeping Letter from the Past—Echo Reading* (page 134) and *Street Sweeping Letter from Today—Echo Reading* (page 135) on the overhead. Read the "then" letter aloud to the class, emphasizing the use of expression. You may wish to read the letter using variations in expressions that make the reading sound unnatural, and then model using proper expressions. Allow students to share their own ideas about the types of expressions that could be used when reading the "today" letter.

3. Tell students that they will be reading the letters using echo reading. Model this for students by reading the first line of the "then" letter. Then, have the students echo what you have read. Do this until you have read the entire letter with the students.

4. Place the students into groups of four. Each group will present echo readings of the letters to the class and their performances will be video-taped. Then, the class will vote on which group read the letters most naturally, using the best expressions. That group's tape will be sent to sanitation departments in the community.

5. Give students copies of the letters, which have been broken into echo reading parts for four students. Assign each group member a part, and allow the groups to practice their echo readings. On the day of the performances, remind students to use proper expressions. Then, ask the students to watch the videotapes and vote on the best performance. Also distribute copies of the *Fluency Evaluation* (page 136) to the students. Go over the evaluation before having students evaluate their taped performances.

Swept Away *(cont.)*

History Connection

Benjamin Franklin started the first public street cleaning service in the United States in 1757 in Philadelphia. Soon, men used pushcarts and brooms to collect the garbage on the streets. Then, horse-drawn street-cleaning machines were used. These vacuums helped pick up debris from the streets. By the early 1900s, the horse-drawn vacuums were replaced by motorized vehicles. Street sweepers with brooms were no longer necessary to pick up the debris that was collected. Now, garbage was picked up and stored in a hopper in the motorized vehicle until it was full. The vehicle would then travel to the landfill where it was emptied.

The first street sweeper was patented by Charles Brooks in 1896. His truck had attached brushes to the front fender that revolved to pick up trash. The brushes could be replaced with scrapers in the winter to help with snow removal. Brooks's street sweeper had a horse cart with no engine on board. The wheels on the cart turned gears or chains. The gears would then drive the brush and belt, picking up the debris. However, Brooks was not alone in his patenting of street sweepers. His patent, and 300 others, were just variations of the street sweepers that already existed.

Vocabulary Connection

Discuss unfamiliar vocabulary encountered in the text. Some possible words are listed below. After identifying the difficult words, discuss them within the context of the text.

- **garbage**—waste; trash
- **hopper**—a container used to put things in
- **idea**—something a person is thinking about
- **invention**—the creation of a new idea or object
- **landfills**—places where waste and trash are taken to be buried
- **machine**—a device used to assist humans in completing a task
- **motorized**—using a motor

Extension Idea

Ask students to write their own letters to sanitation workers in the community. In their letters, students should thank the sanitation workers for the jobs that they do, as well as explain why their jobs are so important to the community. Mail the letters to local sanitation departments in the community.

Sweeping Changes

Source: The Library of Congress

A street sweeper in New York City uses a broom to sweep trash. The year is 1896.

Source: Scott David Patterson/Shutterstock, Inc.

Today, brushes on the bottom of the sweeper truck help pick up trash.

Street Sweeping Letter from the Past—Echo Reading

Student 1

Dear Mr. Brooks,

(audience echoes)

Student 2

I am a street sweeper. I use a broom all day to sweep up trash from the streets.

(audience echoes)

Student 3

Then, I pick up the trash and load it into carts. This is very hard on my back.

(audience echoes)

Student 4

I heard you have an idea for a machine that can pick up the trash. It uses horse-drawn carts.

(audience echoes)

Student 1

I have seen a picture of your idea. It shows wheels that move. The wheels turn gears.

(audience echoes)

Student 2

These gears move a belt that can pick up trash.

(audience echoes)

Student 3

I hope you will show others your invention. It would make street sweeping much easier!

(audience echoes)

Student 4

Thank you,

Mr. Clean

(audience echoes)

Street Sweeping Letter from Today—Echo Reading

Student 1

Dear Mr. Clean,

(audience echoes)

Student 2

I must say that street cleaning has come a long way. It has changed a lot since my invention of the street sweeper.

(audience echoes)

Student 3

My invention used a belt that was moved by wheels. This belt picked up trash on the streets. But, the invention was pulled by a horse.

(audience echoes)

Student 4

Horses are no longer used. My invention was just the beginning of a new world of street cleaning.

(audience echoes)

Student 1

Now, motorized trucks are used as street cleaners. They move much faster than horses.

(audience echoes)

Student 2

The large brushes pick up garbage. It is then stored in a hopper inside the truck. The hopper gets full. Then, the sweeper is driven to a landfill. Here, it is emptied.

(audience echoes)

Student 3

I hope this makes the job of a street cleaner much easier!

(audience echoes)

Student 4

Thank you for keeping our streets clean,

Mr. Brooks

(audience echoes)

Fluency Evaluation

Name: _____

Directions: Listen to your taped performance. Then, answer each question.

I used _____ **expressions when I read.**

My expressions: _____ stayed the same

_____ changed during the reading

My expressions: _____ showed the emotions of the reading

_____ did not show the emotions of the reading

My expressions helped the reading come alive.   Yes   No

I liked the way I . . .

_____

_____

_____

_____

I can make my reading better by . . .

_____

_____

_____

_____

That's Entertainment

Objective

√ Students will improve expressive reading skills by engaging in reader's theater.

Materials/Preparation

- Create an overhead transparency of *Live on Stage!* (page 139). If preferred, print copies of the primary source pictures for students (filenames: actors01.jpg. actors02.jpg).
- Copy *Take Action—Reader's Theater* (pages 140–142) for each student.

Fluency Suggestions and Activities

You may want to complete the history and/or vocabulary activities on the following page before this fluency activity. An understanding of the historical context and vocabulary will help students analyze and read the piece fluently.

1. Display the transparency of *Live on Stage!* (page 139) on the overhead. Then, ask the class the following questions: What do the people in the photo appear to be doing? Describe their costumes. Describe the background/setting in each picture. Allow the students to share their responses to these questions. Then, ask them how the two pictures are similar and how they are different.

2. Now, give each student a copy of *Take Action—Reader's Theater* (pages 140–142). Before reading the script, point out the various punctuation marks throughout the script with the class. Ask them what an exclamation point tells them about how the sentence should be read. How do our voices change with question marks? Review the script with the class, and have them highlight all of the various punctuation marks. You may have them highlight question marks in green, exclamation points in yellow, etc. Tell students to pay close attention to the punctuation as they read, to make sure that they use the correct expressions, in order to make their readings come alive. You may wish to review the use of expressions with the students at this time as well, using examples from the script to show them how particular parts should be read.

3. Tell students that they will be performing scripts for another class. Since there are six parts, you may choose to assign the parts to different students, or you may choose to assign every student a part. If time permits, allow them to perform for more than one class, so that every student has the opportunity to perform.

4. Tape-record the script prior to class, asking different adults to play the parts, reading the script with expression and fluency. Then, read the script together as a class, allowing the class to follow along as they listen to the recording. After that, allow students to choose the parts they wish to perform, or assign them their parts. Place them in small groups with the other classmates with whom they will be performing. Then, allow the students to practice with their groups, paying special attention to punctuation, so that they use the correct expressions.

5. Once students are comfortable performing their scripts, have them perform for other classes.

That's Entertainment (cont.)

History Connection

Acting is a profession that has been around for over 2,500 years. The first actor was a man named Thespis. The word thespian, meaning actor, was derived from his name. Thespis lived in ancient Greece, where he won a contest for writing a play. This is said to be the beginning of the theater.

The ancient Greeks were the first actors. In Greek plays, only one actor was on stage and he said all of the lines. Greek actors wore large masks to show their emotions. The ancient Romans also performed plays similar to those of the ancient Greeks, but the Romans used many actors, as well as props and scenery.

During the Middle Ages, churches controlled most of the plays. They only allowed religious plays to be performed. Then, during the 1350s, there was a rebirth in acting and theater. Playwrights such as William Shakespeare and Christopher Marlowe emerged, making acting a great profession and a popular form of entertainment.

Vocabulary Connection

Discuss unfamiliar vocabulary encountered in the text. Some possible words are listed below. After identifying the difficult words, discuss them within the context of the text.

- **comedy**—a funny play with a happy ending
- **costumes**—the clothes worn in a play
- **forget**—unable to remember
- **movements**—changes in your body location or position
- **nervous**—anxious; uneasy
- **perform**—to act in a play
- **scenery**—painted parts of a stage to show where the scenes take place
- **theater**—a place where plays are shown
- **tragedy**—a play that is sad

Extension Idea

Give students blank sheets of paper. Tell them that that they are designers for theaters and theater actors of the future. How would they design the costumes? How would they design the stage? Would the actors wear makeup or masks? Ask them to draw their own stages with actors on them, showing how they think theaters will look in the future. You may also ask students to create their own theater masks like the ones the ancient Greeks used to wear.

Live on Stage!

Source: The Library of Congress

Actors perform a play written by William Shakespeare. The year is 1795.

Source: Maureen Plainfield/Shutterstock, Inc.

Modern performers dance in a play called *Pinocchio*.

Take Action—Reader's Theater

Characters

Mr. Stage, teacher   Mrs. Act, teacher
Emily   Bryce
Sarah   Brendon

Emily: I am so nervous! I have never performed in front of a big crowd!

Bryce: I know what you mean. I do not want to forget my lines. Sometimes I just wish I could hide behind a mask. You know, like the ancient Greeks used to do.

Emily: Boy were they lucky! They never had to show their faces! They just had to show large body movements! That would be so much easier!

Bryce: What about you, Brendon? Are you ready to perform?

Brendon: I can't wait! I can see it now. All eyes are on me as I say my lines! Does it get any better?

Sarah: I am excited too! But, most of all, I love all of the neat costumes and makeup we get to wear. I am glad that we do not have masks!

Emily: Well, at least I won't be the only person on stage. You will all be out there with me.

Mrs. Act: In ancient Greece, there was only one actor on stage. He had to say all of the lines.

Brendon: Wow! That could be kind of hard. There would be a lot of lines to remember!

Mr. Stage: That's right! They sang in their plays, too.

Take Action—Reader's Theater *(cont.)*

Sarah: Just like we can sing in plays today! But, not all of the songs are sung by one person!

Bryce: Mrs. Act, when did plays start having more actors?

Mrs. Act: Well, the ancient Romans acted, too. They used a lot of actors. And, they had scenery and props.

Sarah: I cannot imagine a play without scenery. I think it makes the play come alive!

Mr. Stage: Acting has changed a lot. It is over 2,500 years old.

Brendon: Acting has been around for that long? Wow!

Mrs. Act: You bet it has! And, for a long time, women were not allowed to act on stage.

Emily: That does not seem fair!

Mr. Stage: No, it does not. But, that is just the way it was.

Bryce: So, what would they do if there were female characters?

Mr. Stage: The men would play them!

Sarah: You mean boys would have to pretend they were girls?

Mrs. Act: That's right! They would wear wigs and makeup.

Brendon: Boy, wouldn't that be fun to watch!

Emily: Yeah! Talk about a comedy!

Take Action—Reader's Theater *(cont.)*

Mr. Stage: The types of plays have changed, too.

Sarah: How?

Mrs. Act: Well, like Emily said, the Greeks had comedies. But, they had tragedies, too. A comedy is funny. A tragedy is sad.

Bryce: I think I would much rather watch a comedy!

Brendon: We still have the same kinds of plays today. Some plays are happy, some are sad.

Mr. Stage: That's true. Plays have changed a lot over the years. But, we still do a lot of the same things, too.

Emily: Like scenery and props!

Sarah: And fun costumes!

Bryce: I wonder if theater actors from long ago got nervous like me.

Mr. Stage: Oh, I am sure they did! I am sure they did a great job, just like you will.

Mrs. Act: That's right! And, I bet their teachers told them the same thing we will tell you.

Brendon: What's that, Mrs. Act?

Mr. Stage and Mrs. Act: Break a leg!

The World's a Stage

Objective

√ Students will perform a song for two voices fluently with changes in tone, volume, timing, and expression.

Materials/Preparation

- Create an overhead transparency of *Theaters Through Time* (page 145). Print copies of the primary source pictures for students (filenames: actors03.jpg, actors04.jpg).
- Create an overhead transparency of *"Theaters Then and Now"—A Song for Two Voices* (page 146). Also, make copies for the students.

Fluency Suggestions and Activities

You may want to complete the history and/or vocabulary activities on the following page before this fluency activity. An understanding of the historical context and vocabulary will help students analyze and read the piece fluently.

1. Divide students into small groups. Give each group either a copy of the "then" theater or a copy of the "now" theater. Then, ask the groups to describe the pictures. Place the transparency of *Theaters Through Time* (page 145) on the overhead. Have the groups take turns reading their descriptions. Then, as they read, have the class guess which photograph is being described. Discuss with the students the similarities and differences in their descriptions and in the photographs.

2. Place the transparency of *"Theaters Then and Now"—A Song for Two Voices* (page 146) on the overhead. Tell the class that they are going to read the song with partners. Read the song aloud to the class, so that they can hear it at least once. Then, point out the lines in bold. Tell the class that those lines are meant to be read together, with their partners. However, the first partner should read "Voice 1" and "Voice 2" should be read only by the second.

3. Give students their own copies of the song. Allow students to read the song silently. Then, choose a volunteer to read the song with you. Read the song together, with you being voice one and the volunteer being voice two. Be sure to read the bolded words together.

4. Tell the class that they are now going to practice reading their songs together, with partners, using proper tone. You may want to explain to them that the tone of their voices conveys the meaning of the words in the song. For example, if the song is a sad song, their voices should be sad and lower. If it is an upbeat song, then the tones they use should be exciting and upbeat as well. Have them use proper tones as they read. You may wish to practice using proper tone as a class by having students read the song in an excited voice. Then, have them use frightened and sad voices, along with other tones. Decide as a class which tone is best to use.

5. Assign students to partners. Have them read the song with their partners, with one partner being voice one and the other partner being voice two. Remind students to read the bolded verses together. Tell them that they will be performing the song on video. When they perform, they can either read or sing the song. Give students time to practice their songs.

6. Allow students to perform the song on the video with their partners. Watch the video as a class.

The World's a Stage *(cont.)*

History Connection

In ancient Greece, theaters were open structures. The theater in the photograph is located on the slopes of Mt. Parnassus above the temple of Apollo at Delphi. The main area of Greek theaters was called the *orchestra*, or "dancing place." It was here that the main performance took place. Today, it is known as the stage. The audience in ancient Greece sat in the theateron, or "seeing place." This area was a semicircle. It had rows of benches made of wood or stone. In the back rows, it was often difficult to see the costumes and masks. However, the acoustics in the theater allowed even softly spoken words to be heard in the top rows. Most of those who attended the theater were adult male citizens of Athens.

Vocabulary Connection

Discuss unfamiliar vocabulary encountered in the text. Some possible words are listed below. After identifying the difficult words, discuss them within the context of the text.

- **ancient**—very old
- **broad**—large and very wide
- **cushioned**—softened with padding
- **entertaining**—amusing
- **vaulted**—domed; a ceiling that goes up in the middle

Extension Idea

Find pictures of various theaters for students to see. Then, ask each student to choose one of the theaters and create a brochure, inviting people to come to the theater to see a play. What is special about the theater? Why is it a good theater in which to watch plays? Have them include this information in their brochures. Have the students also include pictures in their brochures.

Theaters Through Time

Ancient Greeks watched plays outside in the Theater of Delphi.

Audience members today can sit in the balconies or lower seats to watch plays.

"Theaters Then and Now"— A Song for Two Voices

Voice 1

Who doesn't love the theater?
I'm sure that I don't know.
Excitement and adventure
Await you when you go.

Voice 2

Whether underneath the stars
Or beneath a vaulted roof,
The theater is entertaining,
And here I have the proof.

Both Voices

People have gone to the theater
Since old and ancient times,
And actors have shown them
stories
Through dances, skits, and
rhymes.

Voice 1

Old-time theaters were in the open,
While actors the stage did roam,
And people watched their actions
In hard seats of wood or stone.

Voice 2

They sat in a semicircle
In seating broad and wide,
Built into the rocky slopes
Of a mountainside.

Both Voices

People have gone to the theater
Since old and ancient times,
And actors have shown them
stories
Through dances, skits, and
rhymes.

Voice 1

Some theaters today are like that,
But most now sit indoors
With actors telling stories
To people across the floors.

Voice 2

They sit in cushioned armchairs
With a curtain across the stage,
And watch the entertainment
While the actors perform the play.

Both Voices

People have gone to the theater
Since old and ancient times,
And actors have shown them
stories
Through dances, skits, and
rhymes.

It's in the Mail

Objective

√ Students will practice divided reading of a text in preparation for a performance.

Materials/Preparation

- Create an overhead transparency of *Special Deliveries* (page 149). If preferred, print copies of the primary source pictures for students (filenames: postal01.jpg, postal02.jpg).
- Create an overhead transparency of *Being Mailed in the Past—Divided Reading* (page 150) and *Being Mailed Today—Divided Reading* (page 151). Also, make copies for the students.

Fluency Suggestions and Activities

You may want to complete the history and/or vocabulary activities on the following page before this fluency activity. An understanding of the historical context and vocabulary will help students analyze and read the piece fluently.

1. Place the transparency of *Special Deliveries* (page 149) on the overhead. Discuss with students what is happening in each picture. Create two T-charts on the board—one for the "then" photograph and one for the "now." Ask the students to list the advantages and disadvantages of using trains to deliver mail. Have them do the same thing on the second T-chart, this time about airplanes.

2. Read *Being Mailed in the Past—Divided Reading* (page 150) aloud to the students. Model fluent reading, especially the use of voice, as you read. Then, place the transparency of the reading on the overhead. Read it aloud as the class follows along. Do the same with *Being Mailed Today—Divided Reading* (page 151).

3. Ask the class what *voice* is. Tell them that the use of voice shows the mood of the reading. Is it a happy reading? A sad reading? By the use of voice, we convey the feelings and moods of the characters in our readings. Our voices might be low and slower if the reading is sad. They might be quick and squeaky if the reading is scary.

4. Give each student a copy of the two journal entries. Reread them together as a class in a choral reading. Then, divide the class into five groups. Assign each group a section. Also assign each group a voice, such as sad, happy, excited, or surprised. Have the groups practice their assigned sections of the journal entries, using their assigned voices. Then, allow the class to perform the divided reading, with the groups reading only their assigned parts. After the class has performed the divided reading, ask the following questions: Which voice is most appropriate? Does voice change the feeling or mood of the journal? Have the class vote on the best voice to use when performing.

5. Invite postal workers to your classroom to discuss delivering mail. Allow the class to practice the divided reading of the journal entries, using the voice they voted on. Then, after the postal workers have talked with the class, allow the students to perform the journal entries for them.

It's in the Mail *(cont.)*

History Connection

Getting mail from one place to another has greatly changed. Colonists delivered mail by asking friends to carry it for them. Slaves in the South carried mail from farm to farm. To get mail overseas, ships were used.

The first United States Post Office was opened in Boston in 1639. Here, people left letters to be put on ships and delivered to England.

With the development of the West, so came the development of delivering mail to the West. Stagecoaches were used in the 1840s to deliver mail to the new frontier. The Pony Express was developed in 1860 to deliver mail from Missouri to California. Young men on horses would trek 2,000 miles in 10 days. This was a long and dangerous journey.

Then, once the Transcontinental Railroad was completed in 1869, mail could be delivered by train, as seen in the "then" primary source picture (page 149). Steam engines on both trains and ships made the delivery of mail much faster. Today, planes are used to deliver mail quickly both across the United States and overseas.

Vocabulary Connection

Discuss unfamiliar vocabulary encountered in the text. Some possible words are listed below. After identifying the difficult words, discuss them within the context of the text.

- **adventure**—an exciting undertaking; an exciting trip; a thrill
- **deliver**—bring; take something to a place or person
- **saddlebag**—a large bag hung over a saddle
- **steamship**—a ship powered by a steam engine
- **whistle**—an object that makes a loud sound when blown into

Extension Idea

Ask students to mail letters to relatives or friends. The students should request that their friends or relatives respond to their letters, telling about the places in which they live. Collect the envelopes and letters that the students have received in response to their own letters. Share them with the class. Then, map the locations of the letters, showing all of the different places where the letters came from. Encourage relatives to also have other people they know respond, so that more locations can be mapped. You may wish to discuss with the class what they should write in their original letters, explaining the class project. You may also wish to mail the letters for them, or send them home to be mailed.

Special Deliveries

Source: The Library of Congress

A postal worker stands at the door of a train.
He is off to deliver mail! The year is 1916.

Source: David Alexander/Shutterstock, Inc.

Today, airplanes deliver mail to far away places.
The mail can get there very quickly!

Being Mailed in the Past—Divided Reading

Group 1

July 3, 1869

Ahhh! What a day! I woke up this morning in Kansas. I was lying on my owner's desk. And, now, I am off to the post office. I cannot wait to see where I end up next!

Group 2

July 4, 1869

Ouch! Being sorted is not much fun. I get thrown from one pile to the next. I just wish I could see where I will be going. I can't quite read the envelope!

Group 3

July 6, 1869

California! I am headed to California! Wow! I wonder how I will get there. Will it be by stagecoach? Or, maybe by the Pony Express. I heard they can deliver mail in just ten days! Oh, sure, it might be a rocky trip and all. I would be going by horseback. But, I would get to ride in the saddlebag. I am sure it is nice and cozy in there. Oh, I can't wait!

Group 4

July 7, 1869

I can't believe my luck! I am not going to be delivered by the Pony Express at all! I get to be one of the first letters to be mailed by train in the West! That's right! I get to ride a train to California! I am so excited!

Group 5

July 8, 1869

I can hear the train whistle blowing! I am on my way to the West! I can't wait to get to my new owner. I heard it will only take a few days to get there by train. What an adventure!

Being Mailed Today—Divided Reading

Group 1

July 5, 2006

Ahhh! What a day! I woke up this morning in Kansas. I was lying on my owner's desk. Now, with the lick of a stamp, I am off to France! I cannot wait to see the world!

Group 2

July 5, 2006

Ouch! Being sorted is not much fun. This machine does not feel so good on my back. But, it will be well worth it when I am on the plane. I will soon be flying over the ocean.

Group 3

July 6, 2006

Ahhh! Look at the clouds below! And to think, my grandpa had to be delivered by steamship! He was happy it only took 12 days to cross the Atlantic Ocean. I should be there by tomorrow!

Group 4

July 6, 2006

Planes travel so fast! The only way I could get somewhere faster is by email. Through email, I can be delivered in seconds. But, I wouldn't get to do much sightseeing!

Group 5

July 7, 2006

The landing was nice and smooth! Now, I get to tour France in one of the mail carrier's bags. What an adventure!

Trucking Around the Mail

Objective

√ Students will read passages fluently and accurately within a choral-reading activity, focusing on voice and expressive language.

Materials/Preparation

- Create an overhead transparency of *Mail Delivery* (page 154). If preferred, print copies of the primary source pictures for students (filenames: postal03.jpg, postal04.jpg).
- Create an overhead transparency of *Dear Postal Worker—Choral Reading* (page 155). Also, make copies for the students.
- Create an overhead transparency of *A Postal Worker's Response—Choral Reading* (page 156). Also, make copies for the students.

Fluency Suggestions and Activities

You may want to complete the history and/or vocabulary activities on the following page before this fluency activity. An understanding of the historical context and vocabulary will help students analyze and read the piece fluently.

1. Place the transparency of *Mail Delivery* (page 154) on the overhead. Ask the students to observe the two photographs. Then, write *Similarities* and *Differences* on the board. Have the students work in groups to see which group can find the most similarities and differences between the two mail trucks. Ask the groups to share their lists with the class. Record the groups' lists on the board under the two headings. You may wish to point out the differences in the size of the trucks, what is printed on them, and how mailboxes and mail carriers have changed. Discuss the similarities and differences with the class.

2. Ask a parent volunteer to join you as you read *Dear Postal Worker—Choral Reading* (page 155) aloud to the students in a choral reading. Model fluent reading, especially the use of expression, as you read chorally with the parent. Then, place the letter on the overhead. Read it aloud again as the class follows along. Do the same with *A Postal Worker's Response—Choral Reading* (page 156).

3. Give each student a copy of the two letters. Reread the two letters together in a choral reading as a class. Ask the class to list the different expressions that might be used as they read the two letters. Write their ideas on the board. Then, practice reading the letters chorally with the students using the various expressions listed. Discuss with the class which expressions worked best and why. Tell the class to be sure to use those expressions as they read the letters.

4. Place students into small groups and have them practice the letters in choral readings within their groups. Tell them that they will be performing the choral reading with their groups for various staff members at the school.

5. Invite various staff members into your classroom at different times. Then, allow the groups to take turns performing choral readings of the letters for the staff.

Trucking Around the Mail *(cont.)*

History Connection

In 1775, Benjamin Franklin was voted to be the Postmaster General, making him the "Father of the United States Postal Service." This also began the new mail service in the United States. New roads were built and more mail carriers were hired. In the beginning, mail carriers were paid by the people who received the letters. The mail carriers received two cents for each piece of mail that was delivered.

Today, the mail carriers have a route along which they deliver the mail. Some walk, while others drive. Using vehicles to deliver mail began in 1914 with government-owned and operated vehicle services. Though some mail carriers in rural areas may use personal vehicles, standard postal service vehicles are widely used. These vehicles do not have license plates, but instead are identified by blue numbers located on the front and back.

Vocabulary Connection

Discuss unfamiliar vocabulary encountered in the text. Some possible words are listed below. After identifying the difficult words, discuss them within the context of the text.

- **customer**—someone who pays for a good or service
- **deliver**—bring; take something to a place or person
- **logo**—a small design that is a symbol for a company or group
- **mail carrier**—a person who delivers mail; postal worker
- **weather**—conditions outside, such as cloudy, rainy, or sunny

Extension Idea

Show students the "now" photograph of the mail truck. Point out the logo of the eagle on the truck. Discuss with students why that particular logo might have been chosen for the United States Postal Service (for example, it is the national bird or it is quick and swift). Then, give students blank sheets of paper. Tell them that the postal service is thinking of changing its logo. What new logo should they adopt? Have the students design and color new logos that the postal service might use.

Mail Delivery

Source: The Library of Congress

A mail carrier empties a mailbox.
The mail truck waits on the curb. It is the early 1900s.

Source: Steven Good/Shutterstock, Inc.

Today, mail is carried in a mail truck. It will soon be delivered by a postal worker.

Dear Postal Worker—Choral Reading

June 19, 2006

Dear Postal Worker,

I see you deliver mail to my home. You drive up to my mailbox in your white mail truck. I like the blue eagle logo. I know that means there is mail waiting for me!

Sometimes, I put mail in the mailbox for you to pick up. Then, I raise the red flag on my mailbox. It lets you know that there is mail in it.

But, my friend doesn't see a mail truck. Instead, he gets mail delivered right to his door. His mailbox is on his house. The postal worker puts his mail in it. Then, he walks to the next house to deliver their mail.

Thank you for delivering the mail to us every day. You bring the mail, even if the weather is bad. You make sure our letters get to our family and friends.

Thank you,

Jacob Writer

A Postal Worker's Response— Choral Reading

July 12, 2006

Dear Jacob,

We are happy to deliver mail to your house. We have been doing it for over 200 years! Benjamin Franklin was called the "Father of the United States Postal Service." He made new roads and hired mail carriers. He helped start the postal service!

But, we do not just deliver mail. We help customers buy stamps and send mail at the post office. We sort the mail at the post office, too. Then, we put it in our mail trucks to be delivered.

We will deliver your mail in any weather. As we say, "Neither snow, nor rain, nor heat, nor gloom of night will keep us from making our rounds." That is our promise to you!

Sincerely,

Mrs. Sarah Stamps, United States Postal Worker

The Votes Are In!

Objective

√ Students will perform a poem for two voices fluently with changes in tone, volume, timing, and expression.

Materials/Preparation

- Create an overhead transparency of *The Right to Vote* (page 159). If preferred, print copies of the primary source pictures for students (filenames: gvrnmt01.jpg, gvrnmt02.jpg).
- Create an overhead transparency of *"Everybody Vote!"—A Poem for Two Voices* (page 160). Make copies for the students, as well.
- Copies of *Fluency Evaluation Chart for Smoothness and Pace* (page 161).

Fluency Suggestions and Activities

You may want to complete the history and/or vocabulary activities on the following page before this fluency activity. An understanding of the historical context and vocabulary will help students analyze and read the piece fluently.

1. Write the word *vote* on the board. Ask the students what the word means. Then, ask them how people go about the voting process. Discuss voting booths and ballots. Next, display the transparency of *The Right to Vote* (page 159) on the overhead. Discuss the differences and similarities between the pictures. Then, explain to students what it means to have the opportunity to vote and why it is important.

2. Prior to class, give a copy of *"Everybody Vote!"—A Poem for Two Voices* (page 160) to a student volunteer. Assign the student to either "Voice 1" or "Voice 2." Ask the student to practice reading his or her part aloud, as well as the bolded sections. Then, have the student volunteer come to the front of the class. Read the poem aloud with the student. After the reading, place the transparency of the poem on the overhead. Tell the class that you just read the poem with the student using "two voices." Explain that they too are going to be reading with partners. Point out the lines in bold. Tell the class that those lines are meant to be read together, with their partners. Then, the partners should take turns reading the other lines. "Voice 1" should be read by the first partner, and "Voice 2" by the second.

3. Give the students their own copies of the poem. Tell students that they are now going to read their poems together smoothly, using proper pacing. Model this for students. Explain to students that their goal is to read the poem together at the same pace—not too fast and not too slow. To evaluate students' fluency, you may choose to use the *Fluency Evaluation Chart for Smoothness and Pace* (page 161).

4. Assign each student a partner. Have them read the poem, with one partner being "Voice 1" and the other partner being "Voice 2." Remind the students to read the bolded verses together. Tell the students that three groups will be performing the poem over the intercom. The class will vote on which groups will perform. Give students time to practice the poem. Then, allow the class to vote on the three groups that most fluently read the poem. Allow those groups to perform over the intercom.

The Votes Are In! *(cont.)*

History Connection

Citizens of the United States vote for the government leaders who they feel will do the best job. Though voting was once limited to white males, it is now a right that every citizen age 18 and older has in the United States.

Voting used to be done by a paper-based system in which voters marked the candidates of their choice. The votes were then counted, often manually. Paper is still widely used today, with punch card ballots. These cards allow voters to create holes in the ballots to indicate their choices. Machines then use the holes in the cards to count the votes. This method is being phased out in the United States, with electronic voting becoming the more popular method.

Vocabulary Connection

Discuss unfamiliar vocabulary encountered in the text. Some possible words are listed below. After identifying the difficult words, discuss them within the context of the text.

- **allowed**—let someone do; give permission
- **ballots**—the papers on which people place their votes
- **democracy**—government run by the people
- **duty**—something you must or should do
- **freedom**—the power to act or think as you wish
- **honor**—approval, respect, or admiration
- **machine**—a device that does work
- **reigns**—having power or control
- **respecting**—thinking much of; thinking highly of
- **supreme**—highest above all

Extension Idea

- Allow students to hold a mock election in the classroom. You may choose for them to vote for candidates for a classroom president, or you may vote on something silly, such as the cartoon character that should represent the classroom. Whichever reason you choose to vote, set up voting booths using large boxes that are enclosed on three sides. Allow students to vote on individual pieces of paper, or "ballots." Then, tally the votes. After students vote, discuss reasons why voting is important, as well as why it is important to vote privately using secret ballots.

- You may also allow students to create bumper stickers and posters to advertise the election. Discuss historical candidates and their slogans. Then, prior to the election, allow students to create their own posters and bumper stickers using original slogans. Display their posters and bumper stickers throughout the classroom.

The Right to Vote

Source: The Library of Congress

Women vote for the first time in 1920. They put their votes on pieces of paper.

Source: Robert Schmidt/Getty Images

Voters today line up to cast their ballots. They use computers to vote.

"Everybody Vote!"— A Poem for Two Voices

Voice 1

It doesn't happen everywhere
And it hasn't always been.
Some people aren't allowed it—
It's a right they still must win.

Both Voices

Vote, vote, vote.

Everybody vote!

Voice 2

And people in our country
Once had to stand and fight
So that every man and woman
Would have this special right.

Both Voices

Vote, vote, vote.

Everybody vote!

Voice 1

It's an honor and a freedom.
It's a duty and a trust.
Please, don't take it lightly.
Respecting it's a must.

Both Voices

Vote, vote, vote.

Everybody vote!

Voice 2

Democracy supports it.
Each person has a say.
It's a right if we'll just use it,
And right will have its way.

Both Voices

Vote, vote, vote.

Everybody vote!

Voice 1

Whether marking paper ballots
Or working a machine,
The power of the vote
Surely reigns supreme.

Both Voices

So, vote, vote, vote.
Everybody vote!
Vote, vote, vote.
Everybody vote!
Vote, vote, vote!
Everybody vote!
Vote!

Fluency Evaluation Chart for Smoothness and Pace

Student Name: _____

Directions: Check the box that best describes the student being evaluated. If the top two boxes for each section are checked, then the student needs to work on his or her smoothness and/or pacing.

Smoothness

☐ Makes frequent pauses. Sounds out words frequently. Repeats words frequently.

☐ Has several extended pauses. Has several repeated words or sound-outs.

☐ Occasionally pauses or has sound-outs. Occasionally repeats words.

☐ Generally reads smoothly. Has few breaks or sound-outs. Can self-correct.

Pace

☐ Reads slowly, sounding out many words.

☐ Reads moderately slowly.

☐ Reads quickly and slowly.

☐ Consistently reads at a good pace.

Running a Country

Objective

√ Students will read passages fluently and accurately within a cumulative choral-reading activity, focusing on voice and expressive language.

Materials/Preparation

- Create an overhead transparency of *As the Nation Grows* (page 164). If preferred, print copies of the primary source pictures for students (filenames: gvrnmt03.pdf, gvrnmt04.pdf).
- Create an overhead transparency of *Choosing Leaders—Cumulative Choral Reading* (pages 165–166). Also, make copies for the students.

Fluency Suggestions and Activities

You may want to complete the history and/or vocabulary activities on the following page before this fluency activity. An understanding of the historical context and vocabulary will help students analyze and read the piece fluently.

1. Place the transparency of *As the Nation Grows* (page 164) on the overhead. Ask the students how the United States has changed. Create a list on the board of the changes. Then, place students into small groups. Ask the class if it would be easier or more difficult to be the leader of a small country, as the United States originally was, or a large country. Have them list the advantages and disadvantages of both. Then, ask the groups to share their lists with the class.

2. Then, place the transparency of *Choosing Leaders—Cumulative Choral Reading* (pages 165–166) on the overhead. Read the information aloud to the class. Then, read the information in an overly excited voice. Read it once again in a sad voice. Also, read it in a monotone voice. Finally, read it in a voice that would properly show the emotions of the reading. Ask the students which voice sounded best. Explain to the class that the use of voice helps us show our emotions to the audience.

3. Next, explain to the students they are going to practice reading in cumulative choral readings. They will be placed in groups of four, and each member will be assigned a number. Explain that R1, R2, R3, and R4 mean Readers One, Two, Three, and Four. The first reader will begin reading. The next reader will then read with him or her, and this will continue until the entire group is reading the text together. Then, one by one, readers will stop reading, until only the first reader is left reading the passage. Demonstrate this process with volunteers using a stanza from the reading.

4. Give each student a copy of the choral reading. Divide the class into groups and assign them numbers. Have them practice their cumulative choral readings, focusing on the use of voice. Tell them that they will be performing for other teachers.

5. Invite teachers from the school into your classroom. Assign a teacher to each group. Allow the groups to read the text to their assigned teachers.

Running a Country *(cont.)*

History Connection

When the Constitution was written in 1787, a government was formed that included three branches. With 13 states belonging to the United States, the delegates wanted to make sure that all states would be treated equally, regardless of size. By creating the three branches of government, they felt that no one person would have too much power.

The three branches are: the Executive, or the president and his cabinet; the Judicial, which includes the Supreme Court; and the Legislative, which includes Congress. Congress is split into the Senate and House of Representatives, with the number of Senators being two per state and the number of Representatives being based on the state's population.

Jobs of the Executive Branch include enforcing laws and leading the nation. The president also appoints his cabinet to help him run the country. The president is elected every four years. Congress creates the laws. A Senator is elected every six years, and a Representative every two. The Supreme Court makes sure that the laws are Constitutional. Supreme Court judges are appointed by the president. They hold life terms. No one branch has more power than the other. The three branches have to agree on the laws.

Vocabulary Connection

Discuss unfamiliar vocabulary encountered in the text. Some possible words are listed below. After identifying the difficult words, discuss them within the context of the text.

- **amendment**—an item that is added to change something, such as a constitution or bill
- **approve**—allow or accept
- **cabinet**—people chosen by the president to help lead the country and give advice
- **constitution**—a document containing laws that tell how a government should be run
- **country**—a nation
- **elected**—selected for an office by voters
- **government**—the system of people that runs a country
- **leaders**—guides
- **president**—the leader of a country
- **supreme**—greatest; highest

Extension Idea

Ask students to pretend they are writers of the Constitution, but they must create a Constitution for the United States today. Therefore, they would have all 50 states represented at the Constitutional Convention. Would their job be easy? Why or why not? What changes would they make to the original Constitution? How would writing it today be more difficult than writing it with only 13 states belonging to the nation? Have the students consider these questions as they create diary entries, explaining a day in the life of the framers of the new Constitution. Then, as a class, create a classroom constitution, with everyone agreeing on the laws and rights written in it.

As the Nation Grows

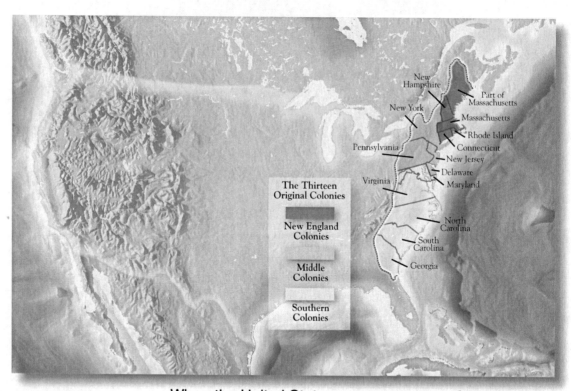

When the United States government was formed, there were only 13 states.

Today, government leaders must work together to help the people in all 50 states.

Choosing Leaders—Cumulative Choral Reading

R1: Our government was formed over 200 years ago!

R1, R2: That's right! The framers were the men who wrote our Constitution. They wrote it in the year 1787.

R1, R2, R3: At that time, there were only 13 states. Each state came together to create the supreme law of the land called the Constitution.

R1, R2, R3, R4: And what a law it is! We still use the Constitution today for all 50 states.

R1, R2, R3: The Constitution helps our leaders. It tells them what the rights of the people are. This is the part of the Constitution called the Bill of Rights.

R1, R2: The Constitution also lets our leaders know that no one can have too much power. The framers did not want a king or ruler in the United States!

R1: That is why they made three branches of government.

R1, R2: The first branch is called the Executive Branch. It is made up of the president and his cabinet.

R1, R2, R3: The president leads the country. He enforces the laws, too. The president is elected every four years by voters. He assigns people to his cabinet. The cabinet members help him lead the country.

R1, R2, R3, R4: Then, there is the Legislative Branch. It is made up of Congress. Congress has two groups. They are the House of Representatives and the Senate.

Choosing Leaders—Cumulative Choral Reading *(cont.)*

R1, R2, R3: Congress makes the laws. Both houses in Congress have to approve them. The president has to approve the laws, too. Senators are elected every six years. Representatives are elected every two years.

R1, R2: The third branch is the Judicial Branch. The Supreme Court is in this branch. Judges of the Supreme Court are chosen by the president. They get to be on the Supreme Court for life. But, Congress has to approve them.

R1: The Judicial Branch explains what the laws mean. It also explains the Constitution when there is a question.

R1, R2: The Constitution has amendments, too.

R1, R2, R3: Amendments were added to the Constitution. Amendments are changes made to the Constitution. One amendment was the Thirteenth Amendment. It said there could be no more slavery. And, the Nineteenth Amendment let women vote. But, amendments are not added often.

R1, R2, R3, R4: Our country has changed a lot in 200 years. But, our government leaders still follow the Constitution. It is the same Constitution that the leaders of the first 13 states followed. So, even as the country grows and changes, the Constitution stays the same!

Scouting Out Ways to Serve

Objective

√ Students will read passages fluently and accurately within a paired-reading activity.

Materials/Preparation

- Create an overhead transparency of *Serving the Community* (page 169). Print copies of the primary source pictures for students (filenames: comldr01.jpg, comldr02.jpg).
- Create an overhead transparency of *A Boy Scout Handbook—Paired Reading* (page 170) and *A Girl Scout Handbook—Paired Reading* (page 171). Also, make copies for the students.

Fluency Suggestions and Activities

You may want to complete the history and/or vocabulary activities on the following page before this fluency activity. An understanding of the historical context and vocabulary will help students analyze and read the piece fluently.

1. Place students into small groups. Give each group either a picture of the Boy Scouts or the Girl Scouts. Then, write *Who?*, *What?*, *When?*, *Where?*, *Why?*, and *How?* on the board. Ask the groups to pretend to be news reporters. They are reporting on the pictures they have been assigned. Tell the students to answer these questions as they describe what is happening in their assigned pictures. Then, allow the groups to share their news reports with the class. Discuss how the reports are similar and how they are different. Display the transparency of *Serving the Community* (page 169) on the overhead. Then, ask students how both the Girl Scouts and Boy Scouts serve the community.

2. Place the transparency of *A Boy Scout Handbook—Paired Reading* (page 170) on the overhead. Read aloud as students follow along. Do the same with *A Girl Scout Handbook—Paired Reading* (page 171). Tell students that it is important to read smoothly. Explain that fluent reading is smooth and the same pace or speed is used.

3. Next, give the students their own copies of the paired readings. Tell them that they are now going to practice reading the texts in paired readings. Allow students to find partners. Have them first read the texts silently. Then, ask them to read chorally with their partners. Remind students to practice fluency as they do their paired readings with their partners, paying close attention to the flow and smoothness of their readings. Tell them that they will be performing their readings for members of the community.

4. Once students are comfortable with their readings, invite community leaders such as Scout leaders, parent volunteers, and PTA representatives, into the classroom. Assign the community leaders to various partner groups. Allow the partners to do choral paired readings of both of the handbooks for the members of the community to whom they have been assigned.

Scouting Out Ways to Serve (cont.)

History Connection

The Girl Scouts was organized in 1912 by Juliette Gordon Low. Today, there are over three million Girl Scouts, including over 900,000 adult members working as volunteers.

The Girl Scouts have a handbook that was first published in 1913. It was titled *How Girls Can Help Their Country*. Today, there are five handbooks, one for each age level in the Girl Scouts.

Boy Scouting began as a training program for young soldiers under the direction of British Army Officer Robert S. Baden-Powell. In 1908, Baden-Powell authored a book for his soldiers. It explained how to administer first aid, follow trails, and find food and water. He also later wrote a scouting book for boys. This idea of scouting was then brought to the United States by William D. Boyce in 1910.

Vocabulary Connection

Discuss unfamiliar vocabulary encountered in the text. Some possible words are listed below. After identifying the difficult words, discuss them within the context of the text.

- **community**—the place you live; a group of people living in the same area; a neighborhood
- **courage**—bravery
- **courteous**—polite; thoughtful of others
- **loyal**—true; trusted
- **mission**—goal
- **morality**—having values; knowing to do what is right
- **motto**—a favorite saying; a slogan
- **obedient**—doing what others have asked you to do
- **promise**—oath; pledge; commitment; agreement to do something
- **respect**—honor; value
- **slogan**—a favorite saying; a motto
- **trustworthy**—worthy of being believed; honest; real

Extension Idea

Tell students to pretend they are in charge of creating new groups for children. These groups will allow children to serve the community. What would they name their new groups? How would the groups help the community? What would the groups' oaths or mottos be? Would the groups have uniforms? If so, how would they look? What would the groups do to raise money? Have the students create posters to advertise their new community organizations, answering the questions on their posters.

Serving the Community

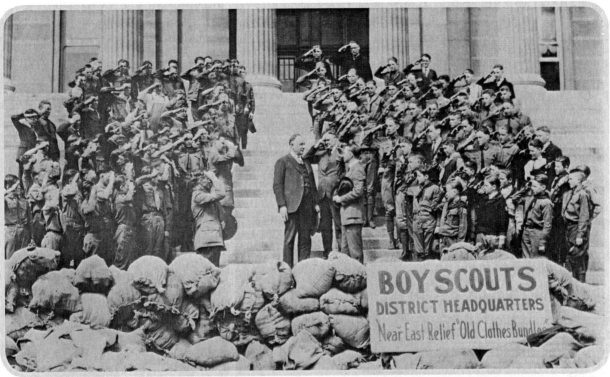

Source: The Library of Congress

Boy Scouts stand in their uniforms. They salute a state governor.
Bags of clothes are in front of them. These clothes were collected for others in need.

Source: David Scott/Getty Images

Girl Scouts meet and sell cookies to former President Bill Clinton.
The Girl Scouts use the money from the cookies to help their communities.

A Boy Scout Handbook—Paired Reading

If you want to be a Boy Scout, you must follow this handbook.

First, you must take an oath. An oath is a promise. It says what you will do as a Boy Scout. The oath says: You will do your best for God and your country. You should obey the Scout Law. As a Boy Scout, you must help others at all times. You have to keep yourself strong. That means keeping your body and mind strong. You need to have morality. Morality means that you will try to do what is right.

As a Boy Scout, you have to follow the Scout Law. The law says you have to be trustworthy. You must tell the truth. You must be loyal. That means you are true to your friends and family. Boy Scouts should be helpful and friendly, too. You must be courteous and kind. You should have good manners. Boy Scouts must be obedient. This means you have to follow rules. Boy Scouts must also be cheerful. You need to be brave, too.

The Boy Scout motto is: "Be prepared." Our slogan is: "Do a good turn daily." That means you should do a good deed every day.

If you do these things, you will make a good Boy Scout.

A Girl Scout Handbook—Paired Reading

If you want to be a Girl Scout, you must follow this handbook.

The Girl Scouts have a mission. This group was created to make the world a better place. There are leaders to help you do this. They have goals for you. Girl Scout leaders want you to have courage. That means they want you to be brave. The leaders want you to have confidence, too. And, Girl Scout leaders want to help you be a good person. They want you to do what is right. That is the mission of the Girl Scouts.

As a Girl Scout, you must show respect for others. You will learn values as a Girl Scout. Your values will help you do what is right. And, you will lead and help others, too. Finally, as a Girl Scout, you will help your community when you can.

As you do these things, you will make a good Girl Scout.

Guiding Others

Objective

√ Students will read a passage fluently and accurately using the call-and-response method.

Materials/Preparation

- Create an overhead transparency of *Leading Others* (page 174). If preferred, print copies of the primary source pictures for students (filenames: comldr03.jpg, comldr04.jpg).
- Create an overhead transparency of *Valuable Leaders—Call and Response* (page 175). Also, make copies for the students.

Fluency Suggestions and Activities

You may want to complete the history and/or vocabulary activities on the following page before this fluency activity. An understanding of the historical context and vocabulary will help students analyze and read the piece fluently.

1. Place transparency of *Leading Others* (page 174) on the overhead. Look at the "then" photograph of the rabbi teaching children. Ask the students what they notice about the picture. Write their observations on the board. Do the same with the "now" photograph of the minister. Compare the two lists. Then, explain to students that religious leaders are members of the community. They help and serve others.

2. Place the transparency of *Valuable Leaders—Call and Response* (page 175) on the overhead. Read it aloud to the students. Model fluent reading, especially the use of tempo, as you read. Explain to the class that when reading, they should use the same pace. Their readings should neither be too fast nor too slow.

3. Give each student a copy of the text. Reread the entire text together as a class. Then, tell students that you need volunteers to read the various parts of the reading. Assign six volunteers parts R1–R6. Also tell the students that the entire class will be reading the lines that are bolded. Have the class practice the call and response several times with the volunteers reading their assigned parts.

4. Place students into groups of six. Assign the members of the groups the various parts to read. Remind them to use correct tempo as they read. Allow the class to practice their call-and-response readings in their small groups until they become comfortable enough to perform the reading. Tell the students that they will be performing the reading for parents.

5. Once students are comfortable performing the reading in their groups, invite parents into the classroom. Assign parents to the various groups. Allow students to perform their call-and-response readings for the parents.

Guiding Others *(cont.)*

History Connection

Religious leaders are important community leaders. They can help the community understand the world around them. There are a variety of religious leaders in the community. Christians have community leaders called pastors or ministers. Catholics call the leaders of their church priests. The Jewish religion has rabbis. Monks are leaders of the Buddhist faith, and gurus or sages are leaders of the Hindu faith. The leaders of the Islamic faith are called imams.

Vocabulary Connection

Discuss unfamiliar vocabulary encountered in the text. Some possible words are listed below. After identifying the difficult words, discuss them within the context of the text.

- **decisions**—judgments; choices made
- **charities**—places that provide help for the needy
- **community**—the place you live; a group of people living in the same area; a neighborhood
- **congregation**—a group of people who have the same faith
- **leaders**—people who guide, inspire, or rule others
- **religion**—a strong belief in a higher power; faith
- **religious**—showing belief in a higher power; having faith
- **valuable**—something useful or having worth; something that is treasured

Extension Idea

After performing *"Valuable Leaders"—Call and Response* (page 175), ask the students to either draw pictures or find pictures in magazines or on the Internet that would show the various ways that religious leaders help the community. Then, write the title *Valuable Leaders* on a large sheet of butcher paper or on a sheet of poster board. Have the students place their pictures on the butcher paper. Discuss the pictures with the class. Then, display the large poster in the classroom.

Leading Others

Source: The Library of Congress

The rabbi teaches young children in 1936.

Source: iStockphoto.com/Sean Locke

Church leaders help others. Today, the people at this church sing hymns.

Valuable Leaders—Call and Response

All: **Religious leaders are valuable. They help the community in a lot of ways.**

R1: They teach the beliefs of their religions.

All: **They teach the community values.**

R2: Religious leaders guide others. They help people make decisions.

All: **They help those in need.**

R3: Religious leaders help with charities. They raise money, food, and clothes for the needy.

All: **They lead weddings and other celebrations.**

R4: Religious leaders visit the sick.

All: **They speak to their congregations on the days of worship.**

R5: They know about the history of their religion. They can teach this to others.

All: **Religious leaders help people find meaning in the world and in life.**

R6: Religious leaders are valuable. They help the community in a lot of ways.

Cumulative Fluency Evaluation

Student Name:_____

Date of Evaluation: _____

Directions: Evaluate the student prior to working with him or her on fluency activities. Save the evaluation so that it can be compared to a later evaluation. Then, use the same form to evaluate the student once again after fluency activities have been implemented.

Place an "X" next to the description that most closely describes the student for each fluency category. If the first and second descriptions are frequently checked, then fluency may be a concern.

Expression

____ Does not make text sound natural. Shows no enthusiasm.

____ Begins to use voice to make text sound more natural. Begins to show enthusiasm.

____ Makes text sound natural throughout most of passage. Shows enthusiasm for most of passage.

____ Reads naturally, with good expression and enthusiasm.

Phrasing

____ Reads in a monotone voice. Frequently reads word-by-word.

____ Frequently reads in two and three word phrases. Reading is choppy. Fails to mark ends of sentences.

____ Reading has a mixture of run-ons and pauses. There is some choppiness.

____ Generally reads with good phrasing.

Volume

____ Tends to read almost the entire text in a quiet, monotone voice.

____ Mainly reads in a quiet, unexpressive voice.

____ Voice volume is generally appropriate, and only occasional expressionless reading is used.

____ Varies volume and expression to match passage.

Smoothness

____ Makes frequent pauses. Sounds out and repeats words frequently.

____ Has several pauses and often sounds out words. Often repeats words.

____ Has occasional breaks in smoothness of reading.

____ Generally reads smoothly. Can self-correct.

Pace

____ Reads slowly.

____ Reads moderately slowly.

____ Reads at both a fast and slow pace.

____ Consistently reads at an appropriate pace.